Entrepreneurial family business identity negotiation

Lucas Byrne

ABSTRACT

The current body of research suggests that the relative importance of business objectives and family objectives changes over time in family firms (Miller et al., 2011). As family firms age, company management tends to provide more resources for the immediate needs of family members rather than invest in projects capable of bringing new streams of revenue. However, there are exceptions from this trend: The decrease in competitiveness does not affect all family businesses. I am interested in how some family businesses are able to maintain a strong business and entrepreneurial focus over generations. I am also interested in the interaction between the family and non-family members that can potentially contribute to creating these conditions. The long history of the family business that was studied in this research project, as well as its strong position among the competitors made this company a suitable case study for the broad research question exploring the sources, the scope and the facets of entrepreneurial orientation present in the family business, as well as the ways in which organizational identity influenced company entrepreneurship and innovation. The results of the study indicate that the company strived to be entrepreneurial, but their efforts were inhibited by the basic organizational pressures and aspects of their organizational identity centered on their being a community retail store. Findings of the study are discussed in the light of the existing body of scholarship on entrepreneurship in family businesses. In addition to that, the study also presents theoretical propositions related to the questions on how and why a transgenerational family business with diminishing entrepreneurial focus may make an effort to foster entrepreneurship.

TABLE OF CONTENTS

LIST OF TABLES

LIST OF FIGURES

CHAPTER 1: INTRODUCTION

Family firms are a significant economic force in the United States and worldwide. There are 5.5 million family businesses in the United States, which account for 63% of employment, 57% of GDP, and create 75% of all new jobs (Kinkade, 2011). Further, family businesses are not homogeneous economic entities. They range in size from small owner-managed firms to large multinational corporations and are found across a variety of industries. Family businesses' prevalence and economic contribution make them a very important source of economic development and growth.

Family businesses create value through product, process, and service innovations that fuel growth and aid in building prosperity. Therefore, entrepreneurial activities are important for family businesses; they increase the distinctiveness of the family firms' products or services and improve their profitability and growth (Zahra, 2003). Thus, it is important that family firms are able to innovate and aggressively pursue entrepreneurial activities.

Despite the fact that family businesses play an important part in supporting entrepreneurship and enterprise development (Pistrui et al. 1997; Aldrich & Cliff, 2003), the entrepreneurship and family business fields have lacked integration (Dyer & Handler, 1994). Indeed, the entrepreneurial contribution of families remains largely under researched (Cruz et al. 2006). Therefore, it is important to examine family businesses as hospitable environments for entrepreneurial activity (Aldrich & Cliff, 2003; Rogoff & Heck 2003).

Family businesses have specific resources and capabilities (Sirmon & Hitt 2003; Dyer 2006) that may both limit and facilitate entrepreneurial activities (Habbershon, Williams, MacMillan 2003; Westhead & Howorth 2007; Nordqvist et al., 2008; Zellweger, Muhlebach, & Sieger 2009). What research has been conducted on entrepreneurship in family businesses is focused on circumstances which foster or discourage risk-taking (Lim, Lubatkin & Wiseman, 2010). There are conflicting theoretical arguments about the influence of family on risk-taking involved with entrepreneurship; this fact suggests the need for a more nuanced theory of family business entrepreneurship. Therefore, studies that take into account the family nature of a firm as influencing both its entrepreneurial orientation and performance are gaining research attention (e.g., Casillas & Moreno, 2010; Pistrui et al. 2000; Mustakallio & Autio 2002; Lumpkin et al., 2005; Naldi et al. 2007; Janssens, Debruyne, and Lommelen, 2011).

This dissertation will focus on family business development, expanding the emerging perspective in the family business literature that is referred to as 'transgenerational entrepreneurship' (Cruz et al. 2006; Habbershon & Pistrui 2002; Habbershon et al. 2003). Transgenerational entrepreneurship examines family contributions across generations and relates it to the company's innovation, entrepreneurship and change. This perspective will help us understand factors that may contribute to entrepreneurship in family business, the input that family members have in shaping organizational identity and entrepreneurial potential of large, multigenerational family business, as well as answer calls for greater integration between entrepreneurship and the family business fields.

Characteristics of Family Businesses

While family businesses are common, an agreed upon definition of a family business is surprisingly difficult. Researchers employ several criteria that help them define whether or not an organization can be defined as a family business. Most of them focus on isolated characteristics rather than identifying the distinguishing characteristics that make the management and employee experience in the family firms unique. These distinguishable characteristics of family firms have been listed by Shanker & Astrachan (1996) as: 1) Percentage of ownership in the hands of the family, 2) Whether or not the family has a voting control over the company (this is slightly different that ownership, if ownership is highly dispersed it is in some cases enough to have only 10% of ownership to fully control the direction of the company), 3) Involvement of multiple generations, and 4) Whether or not family members are directly involved in managing the company as managers. These characteristics, however, are not useful because they focus on relatively superficial elements of the family business. Specifically, they are not necessarily related to how the management of family firms is different from the management of non-family firms.

A better definition of a family firm is presented by Chua, Chrisman and Sharma (1999), who define family business as "business governed and/or managed with the intention to shape and pursue the vision of the business held by a dominant coalition controlled by members of the same family or a small number of families in a manner that is potentially sustainable across generations of the family or families" (p.24). The advantage of this definition is that it emphasizes the importance of the family's vision as a driving force for the business. Additionally, this definition emphasizes that the family sets the goals for the business and, as a consequence, the family is free to choose from an array of goals that it considers important. This may contrast with publicly listed corporations, where company goals are focused to a large extent on generating profit for company stakeholders.

A company in the hands of the family does not necessarily consider economic goals as the most important. Families can have a range of goals for business activity that may have little to do with profit maximization and include objectives that are social in nature. These non-economic goals are often described in the literature through the concept of socioemotional wealth, which is the sum of affective values that a family derives from their ownership of the company. Specifically, socioemotional wealth includes preserving family control (Gómez-Mejía et al., 2007), offering employment and other resources for family members (Schulze et al., 2003b), building the family's reputation (Deephouse & Jaskiewicz, 2013), and supporting local community (Berrone et al., 2010).

Another important characteristic of family businesses is that they consist of two separate, yet comingling, systems, each influenced by a different set of priorities: the family and the business (Carlock & Ward, 2001; Gersick, Davis, Hampton, & Lansberg, 1997). The family system places high emphasis on stability, internal emotional well-being, and the transmission of culture and values; the priorities of the business system include return on capital, efficiency, flexibility, and change.

Nonetheless, the economic and social goals of a family business can create a conflict. The presence of family goals can put a strain on business activities and family business owners are forced to reconcile potentially conflicting objectives. For example, creating new, quality products is associated with expenditures on research and development, which can decrease free cash flows available for family use (Anderson, Duru & Reeb, 2009). Borrowing, often necessary to meet the demands of changing business environment, may come at a cost of losing control over business to external creditors and endangering passing the business over to the next generations (Anderson, Mansi and Reeb, 2003). Similarly, achieving greater profitability might be incongruent with employing low performing family members (Shepherd & Haynie, 2009).

Unlike employees in nonfamily firms, family business members also have the dual roles by being both family members and (family) business employees. This dual set of roles may complicate the responsibilities of fulfilling both family and business expectations (Gersick et al., 1997). Also, the influence of family interactions and potential social conflicts, such as marital discord or sibling rivalry (Dyer, 1994; Schulze et al., 2001), may spill over to family businesses, creating a complexity in family business management.

Family involvement in the business can be also seen as a source of competitive advantage, which can enable family firms to achieve and sustain high levels of performance. Advantages include reduced agency costs through owner control, lengthened investment time horizons, increased commitment to intergenerational wealth, strengthened organizational cultures, lowered transaction costs, higher levels of trust, and more flexible organizational structures (e.g. Gersick, Davis, Hampton, & Landsberg, 1997; Habbershon, Williams, & MacMillan, 2003; Zahra et al., 2004).

Specifically, scholars have begun to identify the attributes associated with the lenghtened investment time horizons that can be directly influenced by the families that own businesses (e.g., Kellermanns et al., 2008; Miller & Le Breton Miller, 2005; Zellweger, 2007; James, 1999). These attributes include the tendency of family firms to have CEOs with longer tenures (Miller, Le Breton-Miller & Scholnick, 2008), intention to pass the business to successive generations (Chua, Chrisman, & Sharma, 1999), investment of their own capital (Sirmon & Hitt, 2003), transgenerational goals (Miller & Le Bretton Miller, 2005), focus on the future and perseverance in reaching organizational objectives (Lumpkin & Brigham, 2011; Diaz-Moriana et al., 2014).

The desire to sustain the family business over generations is a unique characteristic of many family businesses (Gersick et al. 1997; Sirmon & Hitt 2003). Families can thus provide hospitable environment for entrepreneurial activities. The long-term nature of family businesses allows their forward thinking owners to dedicate the resources required for innovation and risk taking, thereby fostering entrepreneurship. Furthermore, the kinship-ties unique to family businesses are believed to have a positive effect upon the recognition of entrepreneurial opportunities (Barney, Clark, & Alvarez, 2003). This may happen because family members are more willing to talk with each other about business opportunities and also have more occasions for this type of exchange of information and ideas. Moreover, owner managers understand that their family business' survival depends on their ability to enter new markets or update existing operations (Ward, 1987; Gómez-Mejía, Haynes, Núñez-Nickel, Jacobson and Moyano-Fuentes,

2007). Additionally, lower agency costs and higher socioemotional wealth attributed to business by family business owners are recognized as strong advantages by creditors of family business (Anderson, 2003). Due to these perceived advantages, creditors of family businesses are willing to offer lower risk premiums for family business loans, thereby improving investing conditions (Anderson, 2003).

Nevertheless, family involvement into the business can also create conflicts. Family business problems include preferential treatment of family members, weaker governance mechanisms and risk-aversion in the form of using less debt financing even at the expense of increased growth, as well as less emphasis on innovation and acting entrepreneurially on the market (Anders, 2008; Aronoff & Ward, 1997; 1996; Kets de Vries, 1993; Sharma, Chrisman, & Chua, 1997; Hall, Melin, & Nordqvist, 2001; Naldi et al., 2007; Miller et al. 2011; Schulze, Lubatkin, Dino; 2003;).

La Porta and colleagues (1999) caution that family wealth concentration in a single business unit may even lead to greater risk aversion, which can have adverse effects on family business development. In addition, the desire to maintain control over business may prevent family business owners from acquiring external capital, often necessary for company growth, because company indebtedness to external creditors presents a danger to family control (Anderson, Duru & Reeb, 2009).

Therefore, it may the entrepreneurial drive of the family business that distinguishes those families willing to take entrepreneurial risks and those who are not. Miller and Le-Breton Miller (2005), as well as Schwass (2005), conclude that the multigenerational family businesses that they studied were able to maintain family ownership across generations thanks to the ability to foster risk-taking and innovation within their organizations. As a result, entrepreneurial drive may be a key characteristic of family businesses that both survive and thrive over multiple generations.

Before we examine aspects of family business entrepreneurship in greater detail, we will first introduce the concept of entrepreneurial orientation and its elements. This general introduction to the concept of entrepreneurship will allow us to better understand its manifestations, as well as conditions for entrepreneurship in the family business.

The Concept of Entrepreneurial Orientation and Its Dimensions

The distinction between the concepts of entrepreneurship and entrepreneurial orientation is close to the one existing in the strategic management literature between the content and the process (Bourgeois, 1980). Lumpkin and Dess (1996, p. 139, italics added) describe this distinction in the following way: "*As the field of strategic management developed, however, the emphasis shifted to entrepreneurial processes, that is, the methods, practices, and decision-making styles managers use to act entrepreneurially. These include such processes as experimenting with promising new technologies, being willing to seize new product- market opportunities, and having a predisposition to undertake risky ventures.*"

The entrepreneurial orientation construct is derived from the strategy-making process literature (Mintzberg, 1973), and addresses the strategy as a set of actions or behaviors that a company enacts in its entrepreneurial strives on the market. Rauch et al (2009) conceptualized entrepreneurial orientation as the entrepreneurial strategy-making processes that firms adopt to achieve a competitive advantage; entrepreneurial orientation is the operational basis for the entrepreneurial decisions and actions (Rauch et al., 2009). Entrepreneurial orientation takes into account not only managerial behaviors and decisions, but also the psychological side of managerial activities; it entails manager's intentions and inclinations toward entrepreneurial actions (Krauss, Frese, Friedrich, &Unger, 2005).

Many scholars (e.g., Covin & Slevin, 1989, 1990, 1991; Knight, 1997; Miller, 1983; Namen & Slevin, 1993; Zahra & Covin, 1995; Zahra, 1993;) agree on three dimensions of the entrepreneurial orientation construct, which include innovativeness, proactiveness toward new marketplace opportunities, and risk taking. Some scholars add an additional dimension of market aggressiveness that captures company offensive responses to competitive threats (Lumpkin & Dess, 1996).

The first dimension, innovativeness, marks the inclination to creativity and experimentation, through the introduction of new products or services or the development of a new technology. It also encompasses all activity directed towards newness, experimentation and introduction of creative procedures that may generate new products, services, or technologies (Lumpkin & Dess, 1996). There are numerous methods by which innovativeness is classified (Downs &Mohr, 1976), however, the most practical and widely used dichotomy is between product-market innovation and technological innovation (Lumpkin & Dess, 1996). Technological innovativeness is focused on the engineering aspects of product development, as well as increases in the technical expertise and the industry knowledge (Maidique & Patch, 1982). In contrast, product-market innovativeness is concerned with new ways of positioning and promoting the product on the market. It emphasizes new value added for the customers, new product design, market research, and differences in advertising and promotion (Miller &Friesen, 1982).

A number of scholars emphasize (e.g., Bernardt, 2000; Johne & Storey, 1998) that innovation in service industry, of which retail industry is a part, has different characteristics than in innovation in manufacturing. They assert that service industry innovation is often non-technological and most of the time involves small and incremental changes in operating processes and procedures. Brouwer (1997) claims that innovation in service firms requires less R&D, investment in fixed assets and in buying patents and licenses than innovation in manufacturing. Atuahene-Gima (1996) underscores the fact that innovation in service firms is more easy to imitate. Also, firms that are innovative and intend to develop new services are more likely to face and be more willing to handle an ambiguous market situation than those who prefer the status quo (Jambulingam, Kathuria, Doucette, 2005).

The second dimension of entrepreneurial orientation construct is risk-taking and is defined as venturing into uncertainty. According to Cantillon ([1755]; 2001), the first scholar to formally use the term entrepreneurship, the major difference between entrepreneurs and hired employees is the uncertainty and riskiness of self-employment. The concept of risk-taking emphasizes the ability to venture in the market using only scarce resources, or venturing with the aid of heavy borrowing (Rauch et al., 2009). Just as in the case of market innovativeness, risk-taking has been the object of many definitions. The strategy field has engendered three broad typologies of marketplace risk-taking (Baird & Thomas, 1985). The first one refers to the aforementioned "venturing into the unknown", the second "committing a relative large portion of assets" and the last one to "borrowing heavily." Entrepreneurially oriented organizations are therefore associated with risk-taking behavior (Lumpkin & Dess, 1996), identified as sustaining heavy debt or making large resource commitments, with the goal of obtaining high returns in the future.

The third dimension of entrepreneurial orientation construct is proactiveness, which involves opportunity seeking and forward looking perspective relative to the market. It encompasses introducing new products or services in advance of competitors, or acting in anticipation of future demand (Kropp, Lindsay & Shoham, 2008). This dimension has also been described as recognition of market trends and exploitation of these emerging opportunities (Kropp et al., 2004). It may also involve inclination to participate in emerging markets and acting opportunistically on the market (Kropp et al., 2004).

In the retail environment, market proactiveness is very important because of the high level of competition among retail firms (Covin and Slevin, 1989). Among retailers, especially, department stores face fierce competition from discount retailers and online stores. Managers who adopt innovativeness, risk-taking and market proactiveness in a retail environment are more likely to develop unique product offerings, that can put their companies one step ahead of the competition. In addition, Griffith, Noble, & Chen (2006) suggest that all the aspects of entrepreneurial orientation, including market proactiveness, in a retail company would allow it to better use its resources and convert them into a competitive advantage.

Lumpkin and Dess (1996) put forward two additional entrepreneurial orientation dimensions: competitive aggressiveness and autonomous action. Competitive aggressiveness is defined by the authors as a firm's strong, offensive responses to combat competitive threats (Lumpkin & Dess, 1996). It is manifested through the intensity of the effort directed at outperforming competitors. In contrast to proactiveness, competitive aggressiveness captures the reactive disposition of a firm.

Autonomy refers to independent action carried out by the management of a firm. Burgelman (2001) defines autonomy as the independent spirit of action necessary to create new venture development, a driving force of entrepreneurial value creation. Autonomous action is relevant to innovativeness, as it is often manifested through the creation of new products or services, as well as to risk-taking, because it involves an element of venturing into unknown.

Entrepreneurial Orientation in Family Businesses

But how can we understand entrepreneurship in family businesses? Stewardship and agency theories present competing hypotheses on how company ownership affects innovativeness and organizational entrepreneurship (Lim, Lubatkin &Wiseman, 2010). Stewardship theory proposes that some managers are intrinsically motivated to put the interests of the organization and stakeholders ahead of their self-serving interests. Agency theory, on the other hand, highlights the rational, self-interested motivations of organizational members (Jensen, 1983), as well as the conflicts of interests inherent within each organization.

Stewardship involves placing the "the long-term best interests of a group ahead of personal goals that serve an individual's self-interests" (Hernandez, 2008, p. 122). Managers display stewardship behaviors by placing organization's interests above their own, thus acting in the best interests of company owners (Davis et al., 1997; Donaldson, 1990). Stewardship oriented attitudes among the company managers (as well as employees) are believed to be necessary to maximize firm performance (Davis et al., 1997; Rousseau and Day, 2012).

Agency theory proposes that the central conflict within organizations is associated with the potential divergence between the goals of managers or employees (called "agents") and owners of the business (called "principals") (Davis, Schoorman, & Donaldson, 1997). While company owners want to achieve the highest possible return on their investment, managers' or employees' goals are focused on achieving personal utility in the form of higher salary, bigger bonuses, or less pressure on the job. This situation may create *agency costs* on the side of the owners: Employees may not be willing to work as hard for the organization, as they could have, if their personal goals were fully aligned with organizational goals.

Situations in which family members' interests are not fully aligned with the goals of the company may be explained through the theoretical lenses of the agency theory. In these situations family members could pursue their own individual or group interests at the cost of company long-term survival and growth, including its innovativeness on the market. In this process, they would extract private benefits of control over the company at the expense of other company stakeholders likely to be present in large family business. For example, family members involved in the business may want to extract private benefits of control, by making company free cash flows available to family members. They may also pursue strategies of conservation, avoiding innovative, risky projects in the name of shorter-term financial security of family members. As family firms age, company management may reserve more resources for the immediate needs of family members, rather than invest in projects capable of bringing new streams of revenue in the future. This type of business strategy focused on family nurturance is likely to negatively impact the competitive edge of the business.

Nevertheless, because there is a high likelihood of family members being in key management roles (Kelly, et al., 2000), goals of the family business owners are likely to be aligned with the goals of the managers (Pieper, 2010; Eddleston & Kellermanns, 2007; Davis, et al., 2010), which in turn increases the possibility of stewardship attitudes present in family businesses. Also, family members are likely to feel the pressure to meet expectations placed on them by other family members. In the family business context, these expectations have to do with contributing to family welfare through work for the family organization, even at the cost of sacrificing short-term individual well-being. Some authors have even referred to family-owned businesses as "high trust" organizations (e.g., Jones, 1983) because they are governed by informal agreements based in large part on emotional attachments and socioemotional expectations, rather than on purely rational, utilitarian reasoning.

Stewardship theorists contend that feelings of autonomy and responsibility drive managers' and employees' motivation to perform (Donaldson, 2008). Consequently, control mechanisms in companies where managers behave as stewards of the business may not only be unnecessary but even counterproductive (Hernandez, 2012). Reduced reliance on formal controls and formal coordination mechanisms increases the importance of a firm's culture as a key determinant of behaviors (Zahra, Hayto &Salvato, 2006).

For all these reasons, stewardship theory has been described as an "ideal" theory for family business research (Davis, Allen, & Hayes, 2010), because it captures the influence of familial ties in family business systems (Pieper, 2010). The conditions expected to be associated with stewardship in family firms include high levels of family identification with the enterprise, shared and aligned values between the family and the business, and an orientation toward the long-term success of the firm (Corbetta & Salvato, 2004).

Stewardship theory helps to explain why family managers may be more likely than other managers to pursue strategies focused on entrepreneurship, innovativeness and company growth. Family business is the source for socioemotional wealth for family members (Gomez-Mejia et al., 2007) including family status, legacy, as well as a basis for personal and group identification. Family members are associated with the company for a long time and on a deeper, more personal level, which makes them more willing to invest in business innovation and renewal adding to the value of the firm. Also, the long-term nature of family firms' ownership allows these types of businesses to more readily dedicate resources required for innovation and risk taking, thus fostering the entrepreneurship (Zahra et al., 2004; Litz, 1995).

Nevertheless, some research suggest that family business managers do not always behave as stewards of their business (Miller et al., 2010; Naldi et al., 2007; Miller et al., 2011). The previous claims that family-owned firms outperform other public companies (Anderson & Reeb, 2003; Miller & Le Breton- Miller, 2005; Villalonoga & Amit, 2006) may be incorrect (Miller et al., 2010) and family-owned companies may be prone to deficiencies in innovativeness and risk-taking (Naldi et al., 2007). For example, based on a study of six European countries, Munari et al. (2010) found that family ownership was associated with lower expenses on R&D. Also Chen & Hsu (2009) found a negative relationship between family shareholding and investments in R&D in the case of Taiwanese companies.

Miller et al. (2011) argued that family owners and CEOs, influenced by family stakeholders in the business assume role identities of family nurturers. In their study Miller et al (2010) showed, among other findings, that the more deeply the firm and its managers were embedded in the family, the less the interests of the firm were protected. This finding in particular may suggest that family managers are not always the stewards of their business.

Indeed, this research evidence suggests that family businesses may possess some characteristics which are at odds with stewardship attitudes. These characteristics may include a culturally engendered, diminished acceptance of organizational change (Dertouzos et al., 1989). That is, change can be seen as a violation of company legacy, or even as an insult to the life's work of previous incumbents. Also, over time, some family businesses may become too conservative and unwilling to take the risks associated with entrepreneurship (Autio & Mustakallio, 2003; Dertouzos, Lester, & Solow, 1989) and that are necessary for company survival and growth.

Family firms may also have difficulty in dealing objectively with a family member's performance and qualifications (Crane, 1985; Gomez-Mejia, Nuñez-Nickel, & Gutierrez, 2001), which may signify a greater acceptance of nepotism or an emphasis on loyalty over professional skills and undermine stewardship. The "privileged" position by family members may cause resentment from nonfamily employees. Further, nonfamily managers may take exception to the implicit immunity that top-level, family executives gain from their family status rather than from demonstrated performance. Family executives may get away with self-serving behaviors precisely because their family positions and company ownership allow them to exercise more influence (Morck, Shleifer, & Vishny, 1988).

Transgenerational entrepeneurship. If the nature of family businesses presents both a potential for entrepreneurship, as well as obstacles ready to undermine it, what are the factors that may contribute to entrepreneurial activity in family businesses? Habbershon and colleagues (2010) propose a theoretical framework of transgenerational entrepreneurship which discusses the factors that may contribute to cross-generational entrepreneurial success in family businesses. Transgenerational entrepreneurship is defined as "the processes through which a family uses and develops entrepreneurial mindsets and family influenced resources and capabilities to create new streams of entrepreneurial, financial and social value across generations" (Habbershon & Pistrui, 2002 ,p. 1). Entrepreneurial mindsets are understood as subjective meanings attributed to entrepreneurship; they take the form of attitudes, values, and beliefs that orient a person or a group towards the pursuit of entrepreneurial activity (Lumpkin & Dess, 1996; Miller, 1983). Entrepreneurial mindsets developed in family businesses which strive to create entrepreneurial, financial, and social value across the generations are an interesting and under researched topic.

Entrepreneurial mindsets present in the family business interact with resources and opportunities for entrepreneurial activities. (Habbershon et al., 2010). That is, entrepreneurial mindsets may not be as effective in a family business that cannot enact entrepreneurial strategies; that is, not all family businesses have capabilities to successfully innovate. The entrepreneurial capabilities entail resources and aptitudes of a given family that may facilitate entrepreneurial activities and create competitive advantage (Habbershon, Williams, & MacMillan, 2003; Sirmon & Hitt, 2003). The presence of entrepreneurial mindsets in a family business capable of enacting entrepreneurial strategies can increase financial, social and innovative performance.

The adoption of a longitudinal perspective acts as an additional facilitator of entrepreneurship in family businesses (Habbershon et al., 2010). The longitudinal perspective necessitates transgenerational value creation for both current stakeholders and future generations. This longitudinal value creation is possible only through innovation, change and growth.

Apart from factors that encourage a transgenerational entrepreneurship orientation, there are also other characteristics of family businesses that may affect family business potential to innovate, take risks and act proactively on the market. For example, Vechiarrini and Mussolino (2012) posit that formalization and professionalization can positively influence entrepreneurial orientation of a family business. In addition to that, family commitment to the business may provide support for organizational entrepreneurship in family firms. Recent literature has particularly explored the positive influence of family commitment to the business on organizational responsiveness defined as identification and rapid exploitation of profitable opportunities (Corbetta & Salvato, 2004; Miller & Le Breton-Miller, 2006; Zahra et al., 2008). Family commitment to the business may also influence other aspects of organizational entrepreneurship in family firms like investments in R&D and competitive aggressiveness, defined as practices aimed at outperforming the competitors.

Overall, families can have both positive, as well as negative influence on entrepreneurship and innovation. Family resources and capabilities may boost family business innovativeness, whereas some family-oriented (rather than business-oriented) considerations may inhibit it. The competing hypotheses with regard to the effects of company ownership on innovativeness and organizational entrepreneurship (stewardship theory vs. agency theory) (Lim, Lubatkin & Wiseman, 2010), as well as the importance of an entrepreneurial mindset for the success and survival of family firms across generations require further research about how families influence their firms' entrepreneurial activities (Salvato, 2004; Nordqvist, 2005).

This research will address this gap in literature by investigating how the interaction between the family and the business affects entrepreneurial orientation of the company and how both family and non-family employees influence entrepreneurial decision-making activities. Therefore, Research Question 1 is:

RQ1: How do family and nonfamily members influence the process of entrepreneurship in a successful transgenerational retail family business?

RQ1a: What characteristics (if any) of the entrepreneurial orientation and transgenerational entrepreneurship are present in the family business and how are they influenced by family and non-family members?

RQ1b: What characteristics (if any) of stewardship are present in the family business? If they are present, how do they influence entrepreneurship?

RQ1c: How does the family enterprise handle the tension between change stemming from innovation and progress and the need for stability, continuity and tradition?

Family Business Identity

It is likely that entrepreneurial activities in family businesses are strongly affected by the way family and non-family organizational members define their organizational identity. For example, the tradition present in a family business may entail elements of risk-taking, constant change, and innovation, or being the best in the market. Therefore, next we will explore the characteristics of organizational identity in the family business.

According to Albert & Whetten, (1985) organizational identity is that which is central, distinctive, and enduring about an organization. Identity answers questions: What is this organization? What is the quintessence of this organization? How is it different from other organizations? Organizational identity is seen as the description of the "essence" of a given organization (Ashforth, Rogers, Corey, 2011). Thus, organizational identity is likely to express organizational goals and values, as well as constitute for organizational members what the "reference point" is for their future activities and cognition.

Multiple organizational identities are likely to exist when there are several different views on what is central, distinctive, and enduring about the organization (Pratt & Foreman, 2000). In addition, multiple organizational identities have both advantages, as well as disadvantages for business' strategies. Multiple identities help organizations address disparate demands formulated by organizational stakeholders, as well as help develop firm's legitimacy (Albert & Whetten, 1985; Pratt & Foreman, 2000).

Nevertheless, multiple identities can also present problems for organizations. Organizational members are likely to experience conflict when multiple identities are fused together. Different values and beliefs embedded in multiple identities may demand contradictory actions on the site of the company (Golden-Biddle & Rao, 1997; Pratt & Rafaeli, 1997; Pratt & Foreman, 2000).

Albert & Whetten (1985) suggest that multiple identities can exist in two different forms in organizations: Ideographic and holographic. Ideographic identities exist when different organizational units assume different identities. For example, different ideographic identities may be salient in a pharmaceutical company: While the research and development department may value knowledge creation, loose controls, and product quality, marketing or sales may emphasize efficiency, tight control and quick selling of goods, even at the cost of customers' well-being.

In contrast, a holographic identity arises when organizational members share beliefs about organizational identity which may entail dissimilar or even conflicting elements, thus potentially creating distinguishable identities (Albert & Whetten, 1985). For example, in Foreman and Whetten's (2002) study of rural cooperatives, organizational members perceived the cooperatives as having two distinct identities – one containing pragmatic and business-focused characteristics, and the other described as normative, communal, family-oriented. As Foreman and Whetten (2002) note, the existence of holographic multiple identities has a positive effect on organizational performance, even though it facilitates the pursuit of seemingly conflicting goals. In Foreman and Whetten (2002), holographic multiple identities helped rural cooperatives to effectively pursue their mission of "common economic, social, and educational aims by means of business" (p. 623) by cherishing family values while achieving economic benefits that could later be used for economic and social advancement of all organizational members.

Multiple identities are likely to be present in family businesses. Indeed, Sundaramurthy and Kriener (2008, p. 415) assert that "family businesses are unique in that two not necessarily compatible identities – the family and business – interact." Family firm's organizational identity may possess the elements of both a family identity and a business identity, which are activated simultaneously on an ongoing basis (Shepherd & Haynie, 2009). A family identity is defined as "the set of behavioral expectations associated with the family role", while a business owner identity is defined as "the set of behavioral expectations associated with the business owner role" (Shepherd & Haynie, 2009, p. 1251). The simultaneous presence of these two identities may create incompatible expectations with regard to family business objectives and cause conflicts within family members as well as between family and non-family employees (Miller, Le Breton-Miller & Lester, 2011; Shepherd and Haynie (2009).

Organizational identity in family businesses has attracted some research attention. However, much of previous research only considers the impact of family members on family business identity development (Dyer & Whetten, 2006; Reay, 2009; Shepherd & Haynie, 2009a, 2009b; Sundaramurthy & Kreiner, 2008). The problem with this approach is that it neglects a large portion of employees in a family business who are *not* family members. Indeed, 80% of the employees in a family business are non-family members (Mass Mutual, 2007). How non-family employees affect organizational identity in large family businesses is, thus, an important and interesting research topic.

Nevertheless, it is the family members who are likely to have the most significant influence on defining the organizational identity of their enterprises; most non-family employees do not have the influence provided by familial ties to strongly influence the most distinctive and enduring characteristics of a family business that form its organizational identity.

Moreover, family members are the ones who struggle to manage simultaneously their public (organizational) and private (familial) identifications. The tension between different types of personal identities (for example: father, boss, neighbor, entrepreneur, business owner, etc.) complicates family business owner-managers' decision making because of the competing expectations inherent in those varying identifications. It is also possible that this tension may become reflected in the most central and enduring characteristics of a family business.

Recently, scholars have begun to examine the role of non-family member employees in family business (Barnett & Kellermans, 2006; Chua, Chrisman, & Sharma, 2003; Carmon et al., 2010; Vallejo, 2008). This research underscores the critical importance of the relationships with non-family managers and employees in large family businesses that have to depend on non-family members for business performance.

However, none of this research has considered the role of non-family employees in shaping the organizational identity of a family business. Their different organizational roles and, possibly, status are likely to affect organizational identity perceptions of non-family employees. If organizational identity of the family business contains elements of "being a family", non-family employees may struggle to find their "place" within the organization. For that reason, research needs to consider how organizational identity of a family business may be influenced by all employees, not just those related to the founding family (Carmon et al., 2010; Vallejo, 2008).

The development of family business organizational identity is likely to affect non-family employees' perceptions and work experiences. In companies where founding family's family identity is strongly integrated within the organizational identity of the family business, non-family employees may be given limited access to managerial opportunities, limited contributions to organizational decision-making, and limited presence on governing boards (Lubatkin, Schulze, Ling, & Dino, 2005; Schulze, Lubatkin, & Dino, 2003). In contrast, if the founding family's family and business identities are viewed as separate, non-family employees are likely to have a larger, more important presence in family businesses (Sundaramurthy & Kreiner, 2008).

Shepherd and Haynie (2009) suggest that family businesses should develop a ''family business meta-identity'' addressing who they are as a family business, rather than focusing separately on who they are as a family and who they are as a business (Shepherd & Haynie, 2009; Reay, 2009). These researchers propose that companies who were able to develop a strong ''family business meta-identity'' are more likely to create a clear sense of identification with the organization and employee commitment where all employees, regardless of their relationship with the founding family, perceive themselves as similar in values, beliefs and attitudes, as well as see themselves treated fairly within the organization (Carmon et al., 2010). Thus, when "family" and "business" identities are merged, the familial types of relationship with their characteristics of trust, commitment, supportiveness and cooperation extend beyond the family members group towards all the employees in the business. Family business can become a "family" for all, not just the founding family members. By developing an overall organizational identity based on the idea of "familiness" extended towards all family business employees, family businesses are able to create a strong sense of cohesion and "buy in" into the strategic company vision and values among all the employees (including non-family members) (Zellweger, Eddleston, & Kellermanns, 2010).

Prior research has advanced our understanding of how the simultaneous presence of "family" and "business" identities can create identity conflicts, as well as shed light on the ways in which family firms resolve them (Kellermanns & Eddleston, 2004; Shepherd & Haynie, 2009; Sundaramurthy & Kriener, 2008). However, there is still a significant gap in our understanding of how the family business identities affect strategic business outcomes (Joshi, 2012). For example, Sundaramurthy & Kriener (2008) urged scholars to evaluate how the different family business identities are likely to influence organizational creativity and learning. These scholars specifically proposed that:

> "The existence of multiple identities may help the family firm respond more effectively to a broad range of stakeholders and enhance its capacity for creativity and learning. On the other hand, the presence of multiple identities may exacerbate conflict, causing the family firm to expend valuable resources resolving these conflicts, or cause ambivalence, leading to paralysis." (Sundaramurthy & Kriener, 2008; p.432).

In this study, I am interested in how the competing nature of "family" and "business" identities and the extent to which owner-managers, as well as non-family employees embrace these identities influences the likelihood and extent with which family firms will have an entrepreneurial orientation. For example, a strong "family identity", involving a strong identification with the family and placing a high emphasis on family interests and perspective on the business, may bind the owners to familial considerations (Shepherd & Haynie, 2009) that can limit the willingness to seek creative input from outsiders, including the ideas of non-family employees. A strong "family identity" may also discourage family businesses from taking risks, because risk-taking may come at expense of loosing family influence over the business. On the other hand, a strong "business identity", which involves the family business being primarily a fully professional- and earnings-oriented enterprise, may make the owners more open to external ideas and opinions; it can also make them more likely to incorporate outsider suggestions into day-to-day business operations (Shepherd & Haynie, 2009).

While "business identity" is more likely to facilitate attitudes concentrated on business growth and development, it is also possible that some aspects of "family identity" may be beneficial in fostering entrepreneurship. For example, family may be convinced that its heritage entails elements of risk-taking, constant change, and innovation, or being the best on the market. Considerations related to of family heritage and legacy may also foster stewardship attitudes towards the business.

The second research question of this study explores how the interaction between the family and the business affects entrepreneurial orientation of the company through the way it affects organizational identity of the business. Therefore, Research Question 2 is:

RQ2: How does organizational identity influence entrepreneurship and innovation in multigenerational family businesses?

RQ2a: How is the organizational identity being constructed by family and non-family organizational members with regard to entrepreneurship and innovation?

RQ2b: How does family identity influence entrepreneurship and innovation in the family businesses?

RQ2c: How does business identity influence entrepreneurship and innovation in the family businesses?

Table 1 provides a listing of all the research questions of the present study along with the concepts that have been explored in the data.

Table 1: Research questions

General research question	Specific research questions	Sensitizing concepts
RQ1: How do family and nonfamily members influence the process of entrepreneurship in a successful transgenerational retail family business?		
	RQ1a: What characteristics (if any) of the entrepreneurial orientation and transgenerational entrepreneurship are present in the family business and how are they influenced by family and non-family members?	• Innovativeness • Risk-taking • Market proactiveness • Market agressiveness
	RQ1b: What characteristics (if any) of stewardship are present in the family business? If they are present, how do they influence entrepreneurship?	• Management as stewards • Decisions reflecting long-term benefit of the business • Values and vision that build the long-term strategy • Personable, kind culture
	RQ1c: How does the family enterprise handle the tension between change stemming from innovation and progress and the need for stability, continuity and tradition?	• Attitudes towards history & heritage of the business • Attitudes towards change & progress

RQ2: How does organizational identity influence entrepreneurship and innovation in transgenerational retail family businesses?		
	RQ2a: How do family and non-family organizational members construct the organizational identity with regard to entrepreneurship and innovation?	Focusing on innovation, risk-taking and market proactiveness.
	RQ2b: How does family identity influence entrepreneurship and innovation in the family businesses?	The characteristics of family identity, family's values and characteristics and their role in innovation, risk-taking market proactiveness and market aggressiveness.
	RQ2c: How does business identity influence entrepreneurship and innovation in the family businesses?	The most central and distinctive aspects of the business identity along with their possible influence on innovation, risk-taking and market proactiveness.

CHAPTER 2: METHODS

In this study, I used a qualitative case method (Eisenhardt 1989; Yin 1994). Qualitative approaches are vital for theory building in emerging fields (Denzin & Lincoln, 1994) such as entrepreneurship in family businesses. Qualitative approaches also aid in the identification of tacit and invisible issues. Thus, this qualitative approach is appropriate for family business studies, which address tacit and complex social constructs negotiated by different actors in multiple contexts (Dawson & Hjorth; 2012; Debicki et al., 2009). It is also best suited for the research problems of this study, which are in the form of 'how' questions (Yin, 1994). Therefore, this research answers calls for the need to re-examine family business dynamics with intense qualitative research including case studies (Heck et al. 2008; Dyer & Marcelino 1998; Nordqvist et al. 2009; Sharma 2004).

The Family Business Case Background

The family business that is the object of this study is *familyretail*, a large department store in the Southern United States. The family has been successfully in operating stores since 1888. Today, the third generation of family members manages the business. Bob and Fred[1], the two brothers currently managing the business started their work in 2004 after their uncle retired. As of January 2012, the company, together with its subsidiaries, was the largest privately owned department store in the United States, with 303 stores located in 16 states. The company generated revenues of $3.7 billion for the

[1] Pseudonyms

fiscal year 2012.

Familyretail sells top national brands of fashion apparel, shoes and accessories for women, men and children, as well as cosmetics, home furnishings, house wares, fine jewelry, gifts and other types of quality merchandise. The company also sells a selection of exclusive private brands focused on offering the customers consistent quality and more differentiated merchandise options. Larger stores may include hair salons, spas, restaurants, optical centers and other amenities. Although the family business operates 93 stores that exceed 100,000 square feet in size, the majority of its stores range in size from 60,000 to 100,000 square feet and are located in smaller towns across the Southeastern United States.

Participants

There are two family members currently working at the company: Bob, chairperson of the board and Chief Executive Officer, and his brother Fred, Chief Operational Officer. Both brothers were unavailable for an interview. I had access to two written speeches by Bob and I have also made notes on his speeches during the period of my work at the company. I interviewed one family member, Bob and Fred's sister, Donna, who worked in the business for 10 years before stepping down from company operations to lead the family charitable foundation.

In order to gain an in-depth understanding of the characteristics of the entreprising family, I also interviewed four employees who worked currently, or in the past, with the family members on a day-to- day basis for at least fifteen years. All of these people personally knew the the previous generation CEO who retired in 2004. Due to their long-term working relationship with the family members, and their long organizational tenures, these people were able to provide an insightful and balanced perspective on the values of the family, as well as its relationship with the business.

There four people were Peter, Michael, Andy (at the time of the interview a retired employee) and Ian. Peter was a sales, marketing and e-commerce executive who had a first-hand knowledge of company decision-making activities. Michael was a long time board member of the company. Andy, also a sales executive, was a member of one of several families with whom *familyretail* family forged early partnerships aimed at gaining additional capital and leadership to open new stores. The relationship between Andy's family and *familyretail* family spanned over 80 years. Andy attended the same family leadership training program as did the *familyretail* family members currently at the helm of the company. Andy's worked in the business for 22 years before retiring from company operations in 2000. Ian, worked in the company Public Relations office for 35 years and had a deep understanding of the history of both the family and the business.

I also interviewed ten upper-, middle- and lower-level company employees, most of whom did not have a strong, day-to-day working relationship with the two family members currently leading the business. These employees' affiliations constituted a range of organizational departments from HR, through buying and planning teams, to the organizational technology. Among these people was one upper-level manager (Mark), who did have a day-to-day working relationship with the two brothers currently manageing the business, but due to his short organizational tenure (1 year) may not have known all the important characteristics of the enterprising family, its history, as well as the values and norms of the organizational culture at *familyretail*.

All the contacts were made through the Public Relations Manager at *familyretail*.

Interview Protocol

I conducted semi-structured interviews with the participants. I used different protocols for family members or non-family members (see in Appendix A and Appendix B.) The interviews were conducted in person. They were tape-recorded and transcribed unless the interviewee did not wish the interview to be recorded (one case). In such circumstances I took extensive notes.

Data

Data included three types of sources: Internal company documents, ethnographic notes collected during 12-month part-time job in the corporate office HR department and interviews.

Internal company documents. I analyzed internal company documents that have relation to company key strategic initiatives. These documents included: brochures, training materials, leaflets, information gathered from internet site pooling employee ideas for improving the business, etc. These sources yielded 259 pages. The documents can be divided into two general categories: (1) Documents created to facilitate company innovation efforts (195 pages) and (2) Documents facilitating organizational change and appraising employees of the changes in the marketplace (64 pages). All the internal company documents were analyzed using same strategies as the collected interviews. The strategies are described in detail in the section: *Analysis Strategies.*

Internal company documents gave information on entrepreneurial mindsets present in the company and the sensemaking process associated with entrepreneurship. They also provided a rich description of organizational identity, boundaries between the family and the business system and how these phenomena affect entrepreneurial orientation of the company. The documents were being gathered with company permission during my graduate assistantship in the company Human Resources department.

Ethnographic notes. During my part-time job at *familyretail* I kept a journal where I recorded observations relating to organizational events and conversations with organizational members. During these occurrences, my role was that of a participant observer. Due to this fact, the initial notes had a form of handwritten scratch notes that were developed into expanded notes from memory outside of my work hours. The expanded journal entries contained the basic journalistic information about the events along with my observations, topics of conversations and some interpretations, if they were presented by the organizational members. I recorded events and conversations that had an important connection to the topic of organizational entrepreneurship and innovation, as well as organizational identity. The expanded journal notes yielded 27 pages.

Interviews. Interviews were in-depth, open-ended and conducted with multiple respondents. There were 15 interviews altogether, lasting from 40 to 90 min.
The interviews were gathered to the point of theoretical saturation, whereby interviews with additional members did not add additional information for understanding of the organizational members' sensemaking. This approach also implied that the interviews were not made with a predetermined number of people.

The average organizational tenure of all interviewees employed in the business was 15.2 years. Interview guides for family and non-family members are presented in Appendix 1 and 2. Detailed information on the interviewees, their role in the company, organizational tenure, as well as the level of association with the family is presented in Table 2.

Table 2: List of interview participants.

Name[2]	Role	Organizational level	Organizational tenure	Notes
Sophia	Training - Buyers and Planners	Individual contributor	15	Not a family member
Heather	Training - Innovation	Individual contributor	15	Not a family member
Eve	Planner	Individual contributor	20	Not a family member
Barbara	Planner	Individual contributor	8	Not a family member
Martha	Development of an IT project	Upper middle level management	7	Not a family member
John	Planner	Individual contributor	17	Not a family member
Larry	Director of Planning	Upper middle level management	Over 35	Not a family member
Nikki	Systems Analyst	Individual contributor	7	Not a family member
Mark	Director, Business Strategy	Upper middle level management	1	Not a family member

[2] Pseudonyms

Diana	Systems analyst for the Innovation Department	Individual contributor	3	Not a family member
Peter	Sales Promotion, Marketing and eCommerce	Executive	Over 25	Not a family member; day-to-day working relationship with the family members
Andy	Retired executive, Sales	Retired executive	22 years before retiring from company operations	Not a family member; day-to-day working relationship with the family members
Michael	Executive, Legal counsel	Executive	19	Not a family member; day-to-day working relationship with the family members
Donna	Family member	Family member working for a family foundation	10 years before retiring from company operations	Family member
Ian	Public Relations	Individual contributor	Over 30	Not a family member; day-to-day working relationship with the family members

Analysis Strategies

To analyze my data, I employed the constant comparison method by Glaser & Strauss (1967). I identified interpretative categories in my data, search for recurring and deeper underlying themes that reappeared in various data sources, and consequently built my interpretation of the emerging themes that inform the research questions. This interpretation was created by coding data into different categories and using interpretive memos to construe the meanings and relationships between different categories. I also conducted a negative case analysis to explore potential alternative explanations of my interpretations. The list of coding nodes is presented in Appendix C.

In order to ensure validity I triangulated my data, conducted negative case analysis, and created mid-case reports that I reviewed with a committee of supportive, but disinterested critics (Lincoln & Gubba, 1985). Data triangulation implies making sure that a theme (or an interpretative category) emerged in different data sources, for example, both interviews, and internal documents. The adoption of a triangulation (Denzin, 1978) of data collection methods and sources within the research strengthens the validity of this research.

The quality review of my emerging themes had a form of regular peer debriefings with a committee of supportive, but disinterested critics (Lincoln & Gubba, 1985). I presented them with my emerging findings in the form of mid-case reports that included evidence supporting my cumulating results, as well as interpretive threads of data needing additional elaboration or clarification using further sources. The committee provided me with feedback on how to adjust the strategy of analyzing my case, or modify my interpretations. These individuals included UNC Charlotte faculty members, as well as peers from a research laboratory at the same university. All committee members had knowledge of the qualitative research analysis strategies.

I did not, however, consult a member check of my emergent interpretations with *familyretail* organizational members, a potential weakness of my analysis strategy. Nonetheless, the repeated presentation of my working results to disinterested critics who knew both *familyretail* and qualitative methods helped me refine my analyses and interpretations.

The main instrument of data collection is the in-depth, open-ended interviews conducted with multiple respondents. The interviews were recorded, transcribed, and analyzed using NVivo (A Qualitative Data Analysis (QDA) software package designed to help coding and analyzing qualitative data).

The data analysis process focused on identifying overarching themes that were supported by interview excerpts to ensure that data interpretation remained directly linked to the participants' narratives, or the wording used in the internal documents issued by the company. The analysis process was executed in four steps.

The first step consisted of open coding, which commenced with reading and summarizing the raw data. Each interview transcript was read sentence by sentence in order to start creating tentative labels for data that summarize participants' narratives. It should be emphasized that these labels were not based on any existing theory, but rather on the meanings that emerged from the information shared by the study participants. Thus, this part of the analysis was inductive, as its goal was to summarize existing data, and develop initial themes. Care was taken to stay as close as possible to participants' experiences, interpretations, and meanings they wished to convey during the interviews. In sum, each important moment or a significant quote in the raw data was given a code. Some of these initial codes were emic, in the sense that they were titled and defined using the words the study participants used in their narratives. These initial codes related to topics connected with the research questions this study aimed to answer, as well as other interesting areas that did not seem, at least at first, connected with the principal objectives of this study that focused on innovation and entrepreneurship.

Once open coding was complete, deductive analysis could commence. Scholars contend that pre-established theories can inform and even drive the coding process (Layder, 1998; Mason, 2002). Hence, in conducting this second, deductive analytical step, the aim was to reorganize codes in a way that would be more helpful to the investigation of the research questions guiding the study. As the research questions related broadly to multiple aspects of entrepreneurial orientation, stewardship, and organizational identity, when examining the data, I focused on themes that could shed light on those topics. Thus, the initial codes were reorganized using sensitizing concepts stemming from existing theories relating to entrepreneurship and family business, which are listed in Table 1. In this process, all sensitizing concepts were used. Another very important objective of the deductive approach was to identify sensitizing concepts that were present or well developed in participants' narratives as well as note those that were absent or underdeveloped. For example, once sensitizing concepts for certain aspects of entrepreneurial orientation were created and applied in the analysis, it was possible to distinguish the aspects of orientation that had a salient place in organizational members' experiences from those that were significantly less important. Consequently, this step aided in better understanding the relative importance of various concepts stemming from extant literature to participants' experiences.

In sum, the first two steps in the analysis process yielded a number of codes originating from the open coding process, as well as the deductive approach employing sensitizing concepts. Many of the codes created using these two approaches overlapped. Therefore, further analysis connecting the generated codes, identifying overarching themes, as well as developing interpretations, was performed.

The third step of data analysis involved axial coding, at which point, interpretations, as well as possible relationships between organizational phenomena, started emerging. Some of the codes generated during the first two steps of the analysis were later subsumed under other codes and relabeled. The rearrangement and reclassification of coded data also involved creation of coding "trees," which contained various subcategories of overarching concepts.

During this stage of data analysis, I also utilized interpretive memos to construe meanings and relationships among different categories. In order to ensure validity of my interpretations, I triangulated data obtained from interviews, observations, and internal documents wherever possible. As similarities and differences across the themes in the data emerged, at this stage, it was possible to identify areas of consensus in response to the research questions, as well as those lacking clarity, or even indicating potential conflicts.

In order to reconcile these potential sources of contention, as well as refine and validate interpretations, the final step of data analysis involved corroborating coded themes through negative case analysis and debriefs with supportive, yet impartial judges. During the negative case analysis, I strove to find evidence of potential themes that could undermine interpretations constructed so far. As a result of this effort, further areas of potential conflict with regard to the final interpretations emerged. Therefore, I sought input of supportive, but impartial experts, whose opinions helped reconcile the differences in interpretations and validate my conclusions. These individuals included peers from the Organizational Science Doctoral Program at UNC Charlotte, as well as faculty members from the same university. During the meetings, I presented to the judges my emerging data interpretations, along with exemplars that illustrated the conceptual content. I also indicated all the areas of potential conflict. The final interpretations, which took into consideration all the data and reconciled the initial areas of concern, emerged after three sessions of discussions.

CHAPTER 3: RESULTS

The Process of Entrepreneurship: Entrepreneurial Orientation

The first research question guiding this study aimed to identify the characteristics (if any) of the entrepreneurial orientation that are specific to a family business and the effect that family and non-family members have on them. Therefore, throughout the results I will provide examples of innovativeness, risk taking, market proactiveness, and market aggressiveness towards company's competitors or demonstrate where they are missing.

Innovativeness. Innovativeness encompasses all activities directed towards newness, experimentation, and introduction of creative procedures that may generate new products, services, processes, or technologies. In the data, this inclination towards creativity and experimentation is reflected in the company document outlining the practices associated with innovation, *The Innovation Playbook*. Here, innovation is defined as "A new idea, or creative adaptation of an idea, that drives sales or profit growth. . . . Innovation is not just problem solving, it goes beyond the status quo" (*The Innovation Playbook*, p. 4). The data also revealed organization's openness towards risk-taking that supports experimentation.

However, data from interviews suggest that only the upper echelons of the organization valued change and generation of new products and services, characteristics consistent with innovation. These findings stemmed from individual interviews, and were confirmed by the analysis of company documents, as well as participant observation.

Analysis of the data revealed that innovation is framed as an activity that helps grow the business and as an initiative aimed at advancing customer services. Indeed, the data revealed that most of the innovation which took place in the company focused on customer service. Customer service is among the company's key priorities, as evidenced by company mission and vision. Consistent with the focus of innovativeness on customer service, innovative insight was defined by the company as "an interpretation, a theme, or pattern you notice that may reveal an unmet need" (*The Innovation Playbook*, p. 36). This statement by the company CEO within *The Innovation Playbook* further demonstrates the importance of meeting customer needs: "With innovation, we will look outside of our company and our industry for trends and insights which influence our business and the lives of our customers. We will use these insights to generate ideas that look and feel different and at the same time improve our business and customer service" (*The Innovation Playbook*, p. 6).

Structural support for innovation. The company employs several structural mechanisms to facilitate and guide innovation. The Innovation Playbook serves as the core document outlining the practices associated with innovation, which is primarily aimed at fostering innovative endeavors. The document codifies in detail the process of generating, evaluating, and testing new ideas that had been implemented in the company. It also provides definitions and categorizations for innovation activities and assigns roles associated with innovation to organizational members.

The Innovation Playbook conceptualizes innovation as a highly organized and continuous process with its own delegated organizational members and dedicated resources. Employees are instructed to use specific tools, forms, and processes associated with the constant "circle of innovation." The definitions, processes, roles, and tools provided in the manual thus serve as a planned and ordered support for the innovation process. The examples for the structural evidence for innovation, meaning the evidence for a coherent organization of the innovation activities, are listed in Table 3.

Table 3: Structural examples of innovation.

Structural examples of innovation	Source	Exemplar
Innovation definitions and classifications	The Innovation Playbook	• Incremental enhancements • Substantial opportunities Transformational breakthroughs
Innovation-oriented activities and events	The Innovation Playbook	• Design initiatives and collaboration opportunities for employees (events aimed at creating ideas meant to solve challenges facing the organization)
Innovation roles	The Innovation Playbook	• Company innovation facilitators at the departmental level, or as a part of working units • Innovation advisory board champions
Innovation organizational structures	Company organizational structure documentation	• Separate Innovation Department • Vice President of Innovation
Innovation tools	Innovation website The Innovation Playbook	An online platform allowing employees to contribute their spontaneous ideas, as well as those generated in response to company "innovation challenges" focused on solving a specific organizational or customer service

		problem • Brainstorming techniques
Innovation measures	The Innovation Playbook	The development of a scorecard for measurement that includes sales and profit growth

It is important to note that one of the employees (Heather) revealed that the move towards innovation in the company was started with a book about innovation at Procter & Gamble read by the third, most recent generation CEO. The book outlined the best practices for a structured, continuous, and reliable process of improvement where external ideas were to be embraced as readily as the ideas stemming from organizational members (from "not invented here" mentality to "ideas can and will come from anywhere" attitude). There is evidence that the ideas present in the book influenced innovation at *familyretail*. For example, *The Innovation Playbook* highlighted the need for sourcing ideas externally (there were targets for the percentage of ideas that were supposed to originate from the external stakeholders: vendors, customers, and other partners). Also, the same source underscored the importance of using extensive customer research information in innovation decision-making, a feature of innovation best practices at Procter & Gamble. Importantly, however, the focus on gathering information from the customers did not receive priority when innovation-focused structures in the company were first created. Company focus was on creating an internal structure for innovation, an "innovation engine" inside the company with allocated resources and a clear path of development for novel ideas.

The use of the structural support for innovation. The information presented in *The Innovation Playbook* specifies that innovation is to be pursued at three levels incremental enhancements, pursuit of substantial opportunities, and the potential for transformational breakthroughs. In this respect, "incremental" ideas are those that take the form of minor changes in existing services or product assortment, and may be implemented quickly. On the other hand, according to company documents, "substantial" and "breakthrough" ideas require testing and budgeting, and are usually more complex and thus require more time to implement. While incremental enhancements are seen as important, *The Innovation Playbook* underscored the necessity of securing funding for "substantial" and "breakthrough" ideas. Hence, it appeared that the company focus was more on pursuing solutions that could prove to be "game changers," rather than making incremental adjustments to existing processes. This interpretation is strengthened by participant observations during area brainstorming sessions (where employees were encouraged to *"think big"* and *"come up with ideas that would get you fired"*). Perhaps the emphasis on "substantial" and "breakthrough" ideas had to do with the strong motivation to implement large, meaningful changes to company processes. It is also possible that while incremental changes might not require large expenditures, the company leaders aimed at creating organizational processes and structure that would secure adequate resources to potentally costly "substantial" and "breakthrough" ideas.

However, despite distinctions being clearly delineated in *The Innovation Playbook*, these were not clearly conveyed to or used by the employees. For example, none of the study participants described innovation as a process with varying levels of complexity or significance. It is necessary to note that the question about participants' knowledge of the *the Innovation Playbook*, as well as the distinctions and rules presented in this document was not asked directly. During the interviews the questions about entrepreneurship, innovation and change in the company were generally worded in such way that the word *innovation* was avoided. This was done with the intention of receiving unscripted answers, as they word *innovation* is currently highly used in the management and innovation is almost universally espoused as a desirable organizational activity. Employee's responses were vague without much examples, or well-thought out explanations how and why the company needs to change, evolve and implement new ideas. Generally, the respondents also did not show much enthusiasm talking about the topics of change and entrepreneurship in the company. Taking into account that the discussed differences between the different types of innovation were a feature of innovation at Procter & Gamble, employees' lack of appreciation for these characteristics of innovation may lend additional credence to the interpretation that the managerial thinking that the company management is trying to implement originates externally and is not created inside the company.

With all of the structural support in place, the organization is able to gather a vast pool of improvement ideas in the form of hundreds of employee posts on the innovation website that was speciffically created to support company innovation efforts. The data analysis revealed that novel ideas are mostly generated during "innovation challenges" provided on the innovation website. This enables employees to respond to pre-determined challenge questions deemed important to the organization and provides the company with an insight into their innovative capabilities. An example of an innovation challenge may be a question: *How may* familyretail *become a top choice for shopping among college-aged customers?*

Innovative ideas are also generated during special employee events designed as brainstorming sessions on pre-defined topics, referred to as area brainstorming sessions. In addition, employees can also submit their ideas that do not originate from portal challenges and employee events. Such ideas are subsequently evaluated by a panel of judges, and those deemed the best are tested in stores using minimal resources.

In practice, however, the number of ideas that employees submitted was so great that only a fraction of them could enter the innovation cycle outlined by the company. In addition, this immense amount of input (hundreds of employee-created posts on the innovation website) generated by the employees made it difficult to provide adequate time to each submission. As a result, many ideas submitted by the employees did not receive feedback or were not submitted for evaluation by the panel of judges.

Evidence against innovation. Although ample structural evidence for innovation existed, the participant interviews yielded limited support for actual innovation. In fact, only two participants, Peter and Michael, discussed the drive towards change and innovation as characteristics of the organizational culture at *familyretail*. These interviewees were high-level company executives and their views, as discusses below in more detail, were in contrast with the prevailing opinions expressed by the lower-level organizational members. While this fact makes it hard to determine the characteristics that may promote an entrepreneurial orientation present in the organizational culture, or inherent in the interaction between the family and the non-family employees, which potentally could be postulated on the basis of the current analysis, this finding is consistent with to the trend of declining innovativeness and entrapreneurship occuring in family businesses (Cruz & Nordqvist, 2012; Laspita et al., 2012).

When asked about company policy on innovation and change, Peter, a higher-level executive close to the family members cited the second-generation CEO, referring to the rapid changes that took place in the business in the recent years:

> *As long as I can remember, the attitude was "We change before we have to," "We are not old-fashioned," "We change on our own terms." But, in the recent years, change has accelerated rapidly. Current leadership encouraged innovation like never before. They want people to take risks, fail quickly and learn from these mistakes.* (Peter)

In this exemplar, Peter suggests a vision of organizational culture in which change and constant adaptation to the customers' needs is an important value for organizational members. This characteristic of organizational culture was, according to him, present during the tenure of the second generation of family members, long before the current generation took the position of business leaders. However, Peter also acknowledges that these postulated characteristics of organizational culture accelerated under the current leadership.

In addition to that, another higher-level company executive (Michael) shared similar views on the topic of the presence of a culture of innovation within the company. These two company leaders, Peter and Michael, clearly demonstrated that they adopted the same attitudes towards new ideas and experimentation as did the previous leader of the company. Nevertheless, the lower level employees did not regard organizational culture of the past to have had those innovation and change-focused attributes.

As previously noted, lower-level organizational members, failed, to comment on company practices that supported innovation under previous company leadership. In contrast, there seemed to be a consensus regarding the unsatisfying organizational change in the earlier years, a shortcoming that has only been addressed in recent years:

> *When the late* Mr. Familyretailer . . . *was still around, and he was running the organization, I think he probably kept things the way he had in the past. Like, I don't think he could have made changes that they're doing now. I don't think the younger generation could have shifted direction with him still there. I think, since his passing, they've been able to make all these changes.* (Nikki)

In this quote, Nikki reminisces about the times before the current generation took the reins of the company, noting that the previous generation had their own way of running the business affairs and was unlikely to introduce changes. This stands in contrast to the views shared by Peter and Michael, as Nikki is clearly of opinion that change was difficult under the previous leadership, who instilled organizational culture that did not promote innovation.

The organizational members interviewed as a part of this study also pointed out the necessity of introducing modifications into their processes and services in response to changing customer preferences and general market environment. For example, a company executive pointed out during a presentation to the employees: *"We found that some of our stores were becoming dated. . . . This information was not just humbling, but scary.*" Heather from the training department, an organizational member with a 15-year tenure, had similar thoughts on this issue:

> *I think everything they're doing has been necessary. Our tools are outdated, majorly outdated. We were lacking in the hierarchy structure that we needed.* (Heather)

Most study participants shared the view that the company's move towards innovation started at the top of the hierarchy. This is supported by the evidence indicating that, even though many employees were engaged in the process of innovation, the 3rd generation family members currently at the helm of the company were the key stakeholders in that process and key people in driving forward innovation and change. In other words, they were the ones who challenged employees to try out new ideas and surrounded themselves with people supportive of change. Barbara, an individual contributor in the planning department, who had worked for the company for eight years noted:

> *It definitely started top to the bottom. Unfortunately, I think it had to start that way in this company. Um, you have a lot of people who have been here for years and years and years, like their whole career has been there; and there's twenty to twenty-five years' worth of it, and sometimes it's hard to get people like that to change their process. um, so it definitely began with a top down of, saying we know we need to change, here are the things we need to go after.* (Barbara)

As can be seen from the above, in Barbara's opinion, changes were introduced by the family members in company leadership positions. She also points to the relative passivity of the employees with regard to change and innovation. She seems to attribute this lack of initiative to being accustomed to a certain way of conducting business. The leaders' inability to perceive changes in the market environment could be stemming from the lack of exposure to different opinions, tastes, and ideas. Barbara ascribes the shift in attitudes to the understanding of those in the leadership position that changes were much needed in the company.

Another organizational member with a 7-year tenure in the upper-middle level management position, responsible for technological development also said:

> *Some things* Bob *and* Freddy *see when they go to conferences or talk to people in New York, other vendors, other retailers, they probably think we should try that at* familyretail, *and they see if it works for them and if it makes sense. And also the people they surrounded themselves with guide them too. The folks that work directly for them may come and say that we need to do this, we need you to support this, we need to make this happen. I think, it's a combination of things. I think, something they try and they say "Let's go try this" and challenge people around them to come up with those ideas and bring it to them to keep us moving and keep us innovative in the marketplace. It's a combination.* (Martha)

In this exemplar, Martha points out that the company leadership actively seeks exposure to new trends, and acts as a conduit between the market environment and employees at *familyretail*. Therefore, the initiatives connected with the organizational change may be seen as originating at the very top and spreading down the organizational chain of command. She also notes that the family members in executive positions are instrumental in assigning change-oriented individuals roles that would ensure that they are in constant contact with company higher management, including the top family executives. These employees also act as conduits and facilitate communication between the top management and lower-level organizational members. She commends them for enthusiastically testing out new directions proposed by the family business leaders, while also making the leadership aware of the various adjustments that need to be created in the day-to-day processes at lower levels. Thus, the family members' efforts dedicated to introducing innovation in the company are made more effective through their collaboration with handpicked, like-minded supporters working closely with company leadership.

Another employee (Diana), an individual contributor from the innovation department, commented on the beginnings of the innovation process within the company, underscoring the influence and importance of the family members. Diana also indicated that openness towards innovation was lacking at the lower levels of company management. Diana shared the following:

> *I think the family members, I think* Bob and Freddy, *you know, they're making the decisions. Bob values innovation and I think that there are*

> *times where other people maybe aren't. Other senior leaders aren't as excited about change and I think that that's where he really comes in as a family member who's the CEO and says, like, "We are going to change, like, we're going to innovate."* (Diana)

Diana is of opinion that it is the family members, especially Bob, who are the champions of the innovation at the company. She observes that a number of employees at the company do not value innovation to the same degree as the family leaders do and need a "push" from the highest management to introduce changes.

When questioned about the organizational "push" towards innovation the interviewed employees offered a wide range of views. Even though employees' attitudes were largely positive, some individuals felt overwhelmed with the increased workload that resulted from technological changes associated with implementing some of the biggest investments. As a result, they felt unable to participate in innovation efforts. As Sophia, an organizational member in the training department, put it:

> *So that, when you start talking about innovation, my head is already spinning. My head's spinning just to be able to do my job correctly, because I have to learn new processes, I have to learn new things, and that elevates the stress level.* (Sophia)

Sophia, an employee working in the training department with 17 years of tenure within the organization, expressed the feeling of being overwhelmed with the rate of changes at the company and the additional demands that these changes place on the employees. She was annoyed by the fact that, even though employees were constantly asked to contribute ideas, because there were just too many of them, the majority of their submissions were never thoroughly evaluated and thus did not have a chance to be implemented. John, a middle-level manager from the planning department with same organizational tenure, further noted on that point:

> *We want to change everything all at one time. Instead of taking slow measured change, we get caught up in the success or get enamored with the change, with hope of what change can bring. So, we do as many things as we can at one time without maybe taking into consideration the pain or the backlash from the change. I think they probably also misjudged the amount of change that people were willing to do.* (John)

In this exemplar, John expresses a similar feeling of being overwhelmed with change and its demands. There is a hint of irritation and blame in his voice as he speaks of the strategies adopted by the highest management. In his view, the organizational change stretches the limits of what he and other organizational members can cope with. In other words, the leaders would have achieved much better results had they been more aware of the existence of such limits and the boundaries of each employee's ability.

Summary of innovation. The data analysis reveals a top-down approach to introducing changes aimed at creating new ideas for products and services. As the interviewees revealed, company's innovation pursuits are predominantly driven by the family members, even though a range of structural mechanisms were introduced with the goal of facilitating the innovation process at all levels. The analysis of the data revealed that the change to the organizational culture as part of the innovation efforts was limited; the interviews revealed that most individuals seemed disengaged from the innovative processes, and could not offer any in-depth explanation on the meaning of innovation for the company or any actual examples of new ideas for goods and services. Importantly, this fact may have to do with the lack of time and the ability to "step back" and understand the current innovation efforts in a larger context.

In addition, some company members feel forced to contribute to the innovation effort, rather than perceive it as an opportunity to test their ideas and be more involved in the creative side of the business. It is necessary to stress, however, that generally employees perceive the current changes promoting more experimentation as positive and needed. They also see the recent changes to organizational processes, products and services offered as necessary to keep abreast of the contemporary market trends. Thus, organizational members perceive innovation more as a reactive response to the current market demands, rather that a proactive, forward- looking activity aimed at shaping the future of the retail consumer goods industry.

Finally, innovation is predominantly perceived as a "project" introduced by, promoted, and to a large extent carried out by those in the highest management positions. It is seen as an important and worthwhile project, and yet, outside of the main day-to-day business activity. It is possible that the the higher-level managers in the company have more time after the completion of their day-to-day tasks to think about the significance and the long-term impact of the innovation for the company. In comparison, the lower level workers may feel too overwhelmed with their daily responsibilities to contribute substantially to the innovation efforts.

Risk-taking

The second component of entrepreneurial orientation is risk-taking, defined as venturing into the uncertainty and exposing oneself to danger in order to achieve a goal. The analysis of data sources used in this study revealed that the company takes a modest approach to risk-taking. Even though the organization has embarked on a mission to encourage employees to take more risks, the practices currently in place are very much aimed at reducing uncertainty. In addition, the messages that the employees receive, though aimed at encouraging risks, make them cautious of the negative consequences of risk-taking.

The drive towards risk-taking is evident in *The Innovation Handbook*, which presents guidelines that underscore the importance of risk-taking. The guidelines hold a prominent place in the organizational strategy centered on innovation and include the several rules the employees should adhere to (summarized in Table 4).

Table 4: Risk taking rules for employees provided in the Innovation Handbook

Risk taking rules for employees provided in the *Innovation Handbook*	Source	Exemplar(s) of implementation in company practices
Recognize near misses	The Innovation Playbook	Not found
Recognize individuals that have taken risks and executed their strategies well, even if the result was unsuccessful	The Innovation Playbook	Company contests where employees submit examples of their most instructive failures
Value and recognize project execution, not just the outcome	The Innovation Playbook	Not Found
Make stars out of risk-takers and innovators	The Innovation Playbook	Company contests where employees submit examples of their most instructive failures

The company's move towards encouraging the employees to take greater risks in their decision-making processes was clearly emphasized in several initiatives encouraging employees to share their biggest, but also most instructive failures. One of the biggest initiatives was the contest *Fail Forward* lasting several weeks and featuring failure stories from company's highest executives. This focus on groundbreaking, risky ideas was also present in design think initiatives with employees during which employees were asked to come up with ideas *"that would get your fired."*

However, the manner in which management encourages employees to take more risks is not consistent. Although the management tries to promote a culture of openness towards risk, the company rules and policies underscore the importance of *"getting it right the second time" and "learning from mistakes."* Thus, many employees are afraid of taking big risks, as they have an acute understanding that their failure would be tolerated only temporarily. Nonetheless, they will still need to prove their value to the company, not through the risky choices, but through the successes that the risk-taking hopefully produces. As Sophia, an organizational member with 17 years of organizational tenure from the training department explained, "*Nobody wants to be on that fail forward list.*" Thus, given the need to produce results that benefit the company, risk-taking choices are particularly difficult for the employees.

However, similarly to innovation, risk-taking was enacted more cautiously in practice. Barbara, a planner with 8-year organizational tenure noted:

> *I think we're pretty conservative. I don't think we take a- we go out on- way out on gambles. I mean anything's a gamble. You pick of a few new stores, they're all a gamble, you know. Will the customer like what you're doing? Will the customer respond? But, I don't think we would be, again, considered very, you know, shoot from the hip, fast moving, kind of risk type business. We're pretty close to the vest, we're pretty sure we're going*

> *to succeed if we go somewhere, we take some sort of expansion move. We usually have a pretty good confidence level that it's gonna work. I don't think anybody considers us, you know, a really super progressive, you know, we're pretty laid back; and if we're gonna make a move, we have a certain amount of assurance it's gonna work.* (Barbara)

In this exemplar, Barbara shares her evaluation of the decision-making processes at the company and the level of leadership's comfort with risk-taking. In her view, the management favors decisions that are carefully considered and planned. In other words, unless there is a high level of perceived certainty that a new business initiative is going to be successful, the management is not likely to undertake it.

Throughout the interviews, risk-aversion was expressed through avoiding excessive financial risks, as well as the need to protect company reputation. This practice was based on reconciling the risk-taking with the long-term orientation of the business. Martha, an upper-middle-level manager with 7-year organizational tenure, who worked on updating technological processes within the company, shared in her interview:

> *I think they are fairly conservative company that they really make sure that they have very healthy balance sheet, you know, that they really have a very strong cash flow, and they wouldn't take risks that would potentially damage that. . . . Not everything we do is on a cutting edge. And usually, we take more of steady less risky course. . . . They have a vision, and they also know their risk tolerance level of what they going to do.* (Martha)

Here, Martha expresses the opinion that the company management prefers not to make overly risky decisions due to the potential financial losses that could result from adverse outcomes. Lack of excessive debt, which can be associated with a healthy balance sheet, and a strong cash flow are the company assets that the family leaders want to guard against ill-considered, risky decisions.

Consistent with this cautious, conservative approach, large investments resulting in significant organizational changes were preceded by long deliberation and consultation with multiple organizational members. Employees were also thoroughly informed about the changes that were going to take place within the company when the organization embarked on the large-scale investment plan in 2009. The long and involved process of change management in the company can be seen as a way to mitigate the risk associated with organizational change and is another example of risk-avoidant practices. Heather from the training department commented on the careful and lengthy process of change management within the company:

> *And they've done a great job of really soliciting feedback from the whole company, of what we think, what are our ideas to be able to shift company, and reposition it for an even stronger next one hundred years. (...) And they realized it was such a big shift that everyone needed to be involved. So, that created a lot more buy-in, and I think that made the change that much easier, um, because we were all involved in it, and we knew where the company was going. And they've always done really well of being transparent like that.* (Heather)

Heather makes a point that, as they introduced the initiatives focused on the change and innovation at the company, the leaders were active in communicating with the organizational members. Consequently, decisions were made after extensive deliberations and consultations.

Several individuals who were not in a managerial position also believed that, at this point, not all levels of management have fully espoused the orientation towards innovativeness and risk-taking. At the same time, the company management had a perception that the employees did not feel comfortable with taking risks and trying out new things. The interviewees noted that, for a time, company management was focused on hiring external candidates for vacant positions, rather than company employees, in a hope of bringing more risk-oriented individuals into the business. Eve from the planning team, who had worked in the company for 20 years, recalled:

> *I think they are getting a little bit smarter . . . seeing who are the risk takers. . . . There was a point a few years ago that I think the company thought that there was better talent* [with regard to taking risks] *outside the company than inside the company.* (Eve)

According to Eve, the leadership was not able to identify the employees willing and capable of taking risks and introducing changes. She hints at the fact that those proactive employees did not receive support and recognition within the company, and were not likely to receive promotions. Eve also explained that the leadership acted under an assumption that, in order to introduce changes, it was necessary to hire talent from outside of the company, as individuals with external experience were supposedly more likely to take risks and keep abreast with the market developments.

Three respondents also noted that the relative cautiousness the company exercised in the past allowed allocating significant financial resources for investments. Having financial resources readily available, rather than resorting to borrowing from a bank, allowed the organization to embark on the current investment spree without the increase of financial risk exposure due to debt. Again, this fact may suggest risk-avoidant approach. As John, a planning team member with 17-year organizational tenure, explained:

> *The biggest thing that helped that is fact that it has been a secure company for 125 years and there is a lot of cash in the bank. We didn't have to borrow or go after things that were risky. We were able to spend money that we had accumulated and saved up. So, even though there is risk, the downside of it, if we got it wrong, isn't going to kill the company. We can take a risk that costs 50 million dollars because we have so much money from our profits over the last years. . . . So, I think that part of being a*

> *family business has allowed us to kind of pool that money and save that money rather than constantly paying it out in high dividends or building things that we didn't need.* (John)

Here, John shares his view that the control of the business exercised by the family allowed it to accumulate substantial funds for possible future use. Sole reliance on company capital was preferred to seeking loans from financial institutions, as it was deemed less risky.

Summary of risk-taking. Several findings that emerged from the interviews suggest that the company has been comfortable in the past with a risk-avoidant strategy. These include the long-standing conservative financial strategy with few investments, the relative unwillingness to borrow money from a bank, the careful and involved process of managing change and making important business decisions, and a belief that many employees with long organizational tenures are not good risk-takers.

Nevertheless, the company leaders are attempting now to encourage more risk-taking in organizational decision-making. This shift is driven by the understanding that the retail environment and customer needs evolve quickly and cannot be addressed effectively without a certain amount of guesswork. The employees, as well as the company leaders, face, however, a dilemma with regard to risk-taking. On one hand, the company is determined to take risks that would allow it to stay competitive in the face of rapidly transforming environment. On the other hand, however, the increasing number of competitors and decreasing margins make it difficult to easily tolerate financial losses from offerings that did not prove hits with the customers.

Importantly, the analysis of the risk-taking practices may also reveal behaviors that can be beneficial to company entrepreneurship. Corbetta and Salvato (2004) note that family businesses that support a stewardship philosophy will "adopt innovative and proactive behaviors that involve calculated risks, but can also significantly improve firm performance" (Corbetta & Salvato, 2004, p. 359). The analysis of the data can provide evidence that *familyretail* engaged in taking calculated risks preceded by a decision process that involved careful evaluation of options. Comprehensive strategic decision making, conceptualized as the in-depth analysis of strategic options (Talaulicar, Grundei, & von Werder, 2005) supports acting in the best interest of the organization espoused by the stewardship perspective, which is also argued to support entrepreneurship (Eddleston et al., 2012). Family firms that adopt a comprehensive strategic decision-making process may be more likely to create an effective assessment tool for new business initiatives, or be successful at new product or service development, which requires careful evaluation of multiple options (e.g., McCann, Leon-Guerrero, & Haley, 2001).

Market Proactiveness

The third dimension of entrepreneurial orientation construct is the market proactiveness, which involves opportunity seeking and forward looking perspective on the market. Market proactiveness encompasses introducing new products or services in advance of competitors, or acting in anticipation of future demand. The analysis of the data sources included in this investigation did not yield evidence of market proactiveness. In fact, most of the changes that the company was introducing were reactive, i.e., a response to actions taken by the competitors. In addition, in contrast to the effort dedicated to the dimensions of innovativeness and risk taking, the company did not have a formal policy defining its approach to either opportunity seeking on the market, or its relationship with the competitors.

In addition to the reactionary approach to market operations and positioning, several respondents noted that the company benefited from being a family enterprise with concentrated ownership, as this allowed it to react quickly to the changes in the environment:

> *[The] family wants things to move very quickly once they make a decision to change something. Once they have vision, they also have the leverage; they do not need to bring multiple shareholders into the fold.* (Peter, company executive with over 25 years of organizational tenure)

In this exemplar, Peter observes that the limited number of decision-makers and the control that the family exerts over the business allows it to move from deliberation to action much more rapidly.

Market Aggressiveness

Market aggressiveness is the final dimension of entrepreneurial orientation. It is associated with the propensity to challenge the competitors directly. Interview data analysis shed light on company's relationship with the competitors and the level of aggressiveness in pursuing market opportunity. All respondents noted that the company did not try to challenge the competitors directly in the past, or influence the market as the first party in a way that would force rival companies to react, even though the management was always very aware of what competitors do. The present research did not gather any evidence that could suggest strong, emotional comparisons with the competitors or emotional reactions to their actions; no shadenfeunde from competitors' failures, and no boasting over own successes. Larry, an upper-level manager in the planning department with over 25 years of organizational tenure noted:

> *You know, I would say we were not usually the ones that go out and do something first. We like to let someone else to do something first and fail . . . or succeed and then we go and do it later. . . .* (Larry)

As described here, in the company, it is customary to base business decisions on market evidence, as indicated by their main competitors' activities. Larry points out that this market evidence is more likely to be gathered through the actions of the competitors, rather than through company's own experience in dealing on the market.

Summary of the Entrepreneurial Orientation.

The current research found limited evidence of the presence of the two first facets of entrepreneurial orientation: Innovativeness and risk-taking. Innovation was a highly structured process introduced by the family members currently at the helm of the company with the aim of revitalizing the business. Moreover, innovation was framed as an activity that helps to grow the business, and also, consistent with the organizational vision, as an activity heavily focused on advancing customer service. Even though many non-family employees supported innovation-focused activities and contributed their own novel ideas to the pool of new business solutions, they struggled with the lack of time and the abundance of organizational pressures that inhibited the development and implementation of new products and processes.

In conjunction with the drive to keep introducing new products and services, the company's management also created programs encouraging employees to take risks and to learn quickly from possible mistakes. Apart from this encouragement towards riskiness, the decision-making in the company was marked with careful deliberation. In an attempt to limit the risks of financial exposure, the company also avoided taking bank loans.

Importantly, the respondents identified several disadvantages to both the innovation and the risk-taking activities. The problems included lack of timely and adequate feedback to all innovation ideas which were contributed in great numbers by the employees, as well as the problems of keeping up with the day-to-day amount of work that resulted from changes in company processes introduced as part of the drive to revitalize the business. The lack of feedback left some employees feeling discouraged. Some employees also felt much too overwhelmed with their daily tasks to devote meaningful amount of effort to company innovation. Moreover, the employees also worried about how the possible failures of risk-taking could impact their careers. Specifically, they were concerned that their employment may be terminated if their unconventional product choices proved wrong.

In addition to these problems the employees deemed the attitude towards risk-taking to be marked by cautiousness in the past. This cautiousness had to do with concerns about hurting family reputation as well as an unwillingness to take too much credit that, if unpaid, could result in losing the family control over the business.

The current research did not identify examples of market proactiveness and market aggressiveness. Specifically, the investigation did not reveal examples of the company attempting to act with a forward-looking perspective on the market, or in anticipation of future demand. The scanning of customers' changing preferences, tastes and needs was supposed to be done on an individual level by the employees responsible for making buying choices, but the company as a whole did not perform such activities. The company also did not try to challenge the competitors directly. On the contrary, the focus was on learning from the competitors through gathering from them the best practices. A few respondents noted that the company management may have had some inferiority complexes and might have felt that their company was not as developed as their competitors.

The Process of Entrepreneurship: The Influence of Stewardship

The second part of the first research question pertaining to the process of entrepreneurship focused on the characteristics of stewardship that can potentially be indentified in the family business, as well as their potential influence on entrepreneurial activity. Stewardship motivation may facilitate the pursuit of business improvement through the development of new projects. However, depending on the understanding of what is best for the business, it can potentially also conserve current status quo or lead to powerful risk avoidance.

A large portion of the material gathered for this work evidences the stewardship attitudes that the family members, as well as a number of employees, exhibited towards the business. Individuals close to the family emphasized the feelings of pride that the family had for the business, along with the willingness to grow and constantly improve it.

> *I truly believe that Bob and Freddy take pride in this company. And they see it as an extension of their family and their history, so they really do ask all of us to take that same pride. Because they own it, we also get to own it.* (Barbara)

In this exemplar, Barbara makes a point that the family members value the company highly. In her view, the enterprise is as important to the two brothers managing the business as is their own family and its historical legacy. Because the company holds such a prominent place in the family members' lives and value systems, its employees feel invited to share in the legacy of this family business.

> *They (the family) make sure that the tree keeps growing. . . . I am sure they have personally sacrificed to make sure the company did work.* (John)

John's metaphor underscores the close, intimate relationship between the family members and the company, which is recognized by the employees. John likens the enterprise to a tree that has been planted by the current generation's grandfather, while their successors nurtured it to allow it to flourish to the present state. Thus, it is not surprising that the brothers currently at the helm of the business are motivated to continue this legacy.

Employees that are unrelated to the family also emphasized that the atmosphere of working at this family business is different from other businesses where they worked in the past. Several employees spoke of the value of developing closer relationships with colleagues, working for a company that cared for the employees, and reporting to managers that were willing to listen to employee voices. Thus, interviews showed evidence of the company providing a sense of community, which was associated with being stewards of the organization. Several interviewees spoke of their appreciation of the company's care for the well-being of the people who work in the business:

> *Definitely, I feel like, I matter to the company, and my opinions matter; and if something is really an issue, they have gone out of their way to make sure there is a structure to hear that feedback and react to things that really aren't working. So, I think that's how, I mean, you really feel like there is a support structure here, and people who are listening, and that makes it feel like a family.* (Barbara)

In this exemplar, Barbara explains that company employees do not feel left alone with difficult undertakings, as they can rely on others to offer support. This sense of joint effort makes the work somewhat easier for their peers and subordinates.

This fact may be seen as an example of collectivistic attitudes whose presence is in line with the stewardship perspective (Corbetta & Salvato, 2004).

Several employees also explained that the company management treated them in a fair way in the past. The employees also appreciated the lack of large-scale employee layoffs during the economic downturn that started in 2008. While caring attitudes and listening to employee voices was valuable for the staff, it also made it easier for the organization to gather valuable ideas for innovation and change:

> *The passion and energy of the whole team makes innovation successful.* (Barbara)

> *Getting into newer* familyretial *associates, people who have worked at Macy's and Penny's, . who do truly come in with a true corporate and not a family corporate attitude, I feel very surprised at the ownership the employees feel to the family.* (Heather)

In this last exemplar, Heather makes a point that the sense of unity within the company is not limited to the non-family employees who have worked in the business for many years. In her experience, even the newly hired employees with corporate backgrounds, and without any prior experience of working for a family business, tend to quickly develop a sense of collegiality and start to truly care for the company success.

Evidence against stewardship. Several areas were identified as a source of evidence against the stewardship in the company—the treatment of employees, the high feeling of nepotism, and the lack of proper employee evaluations systems that were present in the past.

Specifically, one employee was not fully convinced of the caring attitudes towards the workers. Heather, from the training department, explained that she witnessed examples of employees who had performed in line with the company expectations for a long time, but were nonetheless fired for not being able to achieve their revenue objectives. She also explained that there have been very limited considerations for lateral moves within the company for employees with good skills, for whom the current job was not the best fit.

> *There will be examples where people have worked in the company for a very, very, very long time and there were no hesitations seemingly to let them go.* (Heather)

Here, Heather, a human resources employee that, due to her position, has insight into the career stories of terminated employees, ponders a possibility that the caring culture may sometimes obscure the arms-length relationships rooted in the hard economic calculation.

Another employee from the planning department voiced her concerns about being able to maintain her employment, even though she has worked in the company for about 20 years, has been an exemplary employee, and has made the company "*a lot of money in the past*":

> *The way I am going this year, I am going to have a bad year. It's my first one in five. I think I have a grace period for this year. If I had two bad years, I am going to start getting a little concerned. But I don't know, since they know my history, I could be safe. It's tough.* (Eve)

In this exemplar, Eve, a planner with a long organizational tenure, reflects on her perspectives regarding security of her position within company. She points out that, if she does not improve her performance in the coming year, her job may be on the line. In other words, despite the overall good performance throughout her long career at *familyretail*, there is no guarantee that she will not be fired.

Another respondent with 15-year organizational tenure raised some concerns related to the transparency with employee hiring, performance evaluations, and promotions. In her view, the company was not always objective and impartial: "*it* [the relationships within the Company] *was too personal and emotional*" (Heather). Moreover, the employee performance assessment was conducted in a way that lacked transparency and employees were not receiving proper feedback on their work. The interviewees also shared that conversations about employee performance were typically carried out during closed meetings attended solely by the company management, and the content of these conversations was generally not released to the workers.

> *I think, in the past 8 to 10 years, it is just the business that just happens to help family owners. Prior to that, in all of the different divisions, that there was a high feeling of nepotism in relationship-based hiring and promotions in the company.*
>
> (Heather, training department, 15-year organizational tenure)

In this exemplar, Heather reflects on the changes to business management practices that she witnessed during her career at *familyretail*. She sees the current management practices as much more merit driven than in the past, which may point to resurgence of stewardship attitudes aimed at safeguarding the success of the enterprise after a period of low occurrence.

This approach changed, however, when the third generation of family members took over the reins of the company. The employees started receiving regular, open, and detailed feedback on their work, which focused on their strengths, weaknesses, and the promotion potential. In addition, the employees noted that, with the change of leadership, the atmosphere became less fraught with personal considerations and emotions.

Summary of stewardship. The family members currently at the helm of the company are proud of the business and they are ready to work hard to see the business grow and develop. In order to strengthen their business, stewardship motivation prompted family members to introduce changes aimed at business improvement. This interpretation may be strengthened by the findings associated with the origins of innovation activities at the company. Before the "push" for innovation was undertaken, family members realized how outdated company processes were and feared for business survival. Thus, in this context, both the innovation-focused initiatives, as well as the risk-taking promotion among the employees, may be seen as facilitated by stewardship that is the will to act in the best interest of the business.

The handling of the tradition and change. The material gathered as a part of the research process provided an insight into the strategies the company adopts in order to handle stability and tradition on the one hand and change on the other. When discussing this topic, the interviewees emphasized an attempt to keep a balance between the two through careful examination of the available options, and slow progress of change:

> *They still are constantly focused on keeping things from getting out of hand. They don't want it to just fly off a handle and be too much for everyone to take in. Like always, they're right in the middle with everything.* (Heather)

Here, Heather makes a point that the company leaders see the need to monitor and manage organizational change, so that it does not become overwhelming or destructive to the organization.

In addition, with regard to the balance between the change and tradition, the company seems to opt for change, but on its own terms, as indicated by the following comment:

> *We want to be the best we can be.* (Donna)

Donna, a family member, refers here to the ambition and drive that the family members have to improve the business. Her choice of words seems to point to the fact that the goal of the business is not to be the best in the absolute terms, but to improve the company building upon its current characteristics. Consequently, business development can create a better version of "us", meaning the company, but not a completely new business entity with a different organizational identity.

Also the following quote emphasizes the company's willingness to change "on its own terms," along with its sensitivity to being perceived as an important and legitimate company in the industry:

> *I think they want to be respected in the retail industry . . . and lot of times I think they have been envious of the larger companies and they want to be perceived as powerful or big as some of the other companies. But, at the same time, they want to do it their own way.* (John)

In this exemplar, John points out that the company management wants to make the changes in accordance with their own vision for the business.

The Process of Entrepreneurship: Organizational Identity

To answer Research question 2, we now turn to organizational identity. Organizational identity pertains to values and norms that central, distinctive, and enduring about an organization. When defining identity, it is usually beneficial to consider the following questions: What is this organization? What is the quintessence of this organization? How is it different from other organizations? Organizational identity is sometimes described as the "essence" of a given organization (Ashforth, Rogers, & Corey, 2011). Accordingly, it is likely to express the organizational goals and values, as well as constitute "reference point" for all organizational activities, including entrepreneurship. The second research question guiding this study explored the effect of the family and the business identities on the entrepreneurial orientation of the company.

Family identity. Based on the interviews with individuals close to the family, including those who knew the previous generation of leadership at the company, it was possible to identify the characteristics of the family identity, as well as understand the influence of that identity on the entrepreneurial activity.

Interview participants reported that the family members were approachable, down to earth, hard working, and humble. Approachability and modesty as the values of the family business have also been seen as reflected in the change of the company logo. Although the family name is still prominent, the company logo changed to *familyretail*, deliberately choosing lower case letters to reflect the shift in company attitudes. One interviewee explained that, in his view, the relative ease with which the family was able to play down its family name in the business title reflected their humility and unpretentiousness. Several employees also noted that the discussed values were applied in the day-to-day behavior of the family members working in the business:

> *The pride that they speak of for the company never feels like they are speaking about pride for their family name and really feels like pride for the company itself. I have never heard any of them refer to it is "my company," "your family company" or anything like that. They always refer to it as if* familyretail *was not their last name.*
> (John, planning department, 17 years with the company)

Peter, a company executive with over 25 years of organizational tenure, described the characteristics of the enterprising family:

> *Lower case in* familyretail *is meant to be more welcoming, approachable. . . . Their* [the family] *value system permeates the organization. It is in how they conduct themselves. They are not flashy; their ideal is being humble servants. It has religious roots. The family has strong religious beliefs . . . is very proud of their rich heritage. Their value is honest hard work. They empower managers and associates. Family value is also great customer care.* (Peter)

The family is well known in the Carolinas, where it sponsors a number of educational endeavors providing significant donations to local schools and colleges. One of *familyretail's* former CEOs also served as a mayor of the city where the company is headquartered for several terms. The family enjoyed a high social status in the local area and thus it is perhaps not surprising that the individuals close to the family emphasized a strong emotional connection and feelings of pride that the family members had for the achievements of their predecessors:

> *I think maybe it's family pride or pride in where we've come from , you know, 125 years... there's not many corporations, let alone retail corporations that have been around for 125 years. So I'm sure they feel that, you know I feel a certain amount of pride.* (Larry)

The interviewed employees also reported that the family has a strong drive to develop and improve the enterprise. They were also convinced of the high levels of ambition of the family members currently managing the company. The following quotes speak to the drive and ambition of the family members:

> *We want to be the best we can be.* (Diana, a family member)

> *I know that - that their* [the family] *desire to- to make* familyretail *brand the best brand in the name of retail is what drives them. . . . It's their family values and their desire to continually improve. I really believe that, because you're right, they could have sold off, made a fortune, and traveled the world. But the two gentlemen who run the company were brought up on hard work and values, and you're not gonna find one person in the community that says that-that their not committed. And they're the hardest working people you've ever met. I've never seen anyone work as hard as these two have. . . . They take pride in succeeding and being the best in the best.*
> (Mark, Company executive, with one year of tenure with the company)

> *Are we so competitive because that's what our leadership is.*
> (Sophia, member of the training team, 15 years with the company)

Family members did not emphasize their ownership of the company. Their approach was more that of being the guardians, or the servants of the business. In addition, the respondents did not perceive the family dynamics as influencing the business decision-making that took place in the new company structure, even though this was not the case in the past.

> *I think it's like a tree that their great great grandfather planted it and they water it every day to make sure that the tree grows. . . . They are proud of the tree . . . not proud because it's their tree. . . . They make sure the tree keeps growing. . . . Most family-run businesses, you know, if it's successful, then it becomes a big ego driver for the, whichever family member is in charge. And it's, as long as I've been around it's never been that way.*
>
> (John, planning team, 17 years with the company)

As described here, in John's view, family identity contains elements of being stewards of the business. According to the aforementioned tree metaphor he used to explain how the family views the company, business is more of an obligation than an asset for the family members. Consequently, their management approach is more that of stewards than of beneficiaries of the enterprise.

Business identity. The company mission and vision that were introduced by the third generation leadership are important parts of the business identity. The company mission underscores satisfying "*modern Southern lifestyle like no one else, so that our customers get the fashion they desire and the value they deserve.*" The vision postulates: "*For the modern Southern woman to count on familyretail first.*" Both company mission and vision underscore the importance of service provided to the clients. Specifically, the mission focuses on delivering quality products for a good price (customers receive good value) and creates a distinct business identity associated with the southern United States.

During the interviews, several employees revealed that the business identity was seen by them as very professional, with high competitiveness and high responsibility placed on all employees, including the family members. In addition, family dynamics were no longer seen as influencing the business, which was the case in the past, before the new generation took charge of the company. Finally, the fact that the name of the business was derived from the family name is not seen as a noteworthy factor: "*It's just that their last name is familyretail.<Laughter> It's really the same [as in other companies I worked before]"*(Martha, upper-middle level manager responsible for technological development). The following quotes illustrate these findings:

> *I think, in the past 8 to 10 years, it is just the business that just happens to help family owners. Prior to that, in all of the different divisions, that there was a high feeling of nepotism in relationship-based hiring and promotions in the company.*
>
> (Heather, training department, 15-year organizational tenure)

> *I think that, in things like that, you know, that's a family business, like, he is a family member. But, it's not like the family all sits down together and decides the business decisions. It's a business. It's a company, so they run it as such".*
>
> (Diana, innovation department, 3-year organizational tenure)

Several interviewees noted that the atmosphere at the company was more relaxed than in other non-family organizations they had had previously worked in. Nevertheless, there was still a feeling of strong accountability for all the actions:

> *I think they are probably right in the middle between personal and professional. Um, people are really encouraged to be themselves and take ownership of things. But, at the same time, I think they want us to be on that professional level where we are holding ourselves to the same level as any other company. Um, but definitely high responsibility. . . . Familyretail definitely expects a lot out of their people; and they're going to give you the responsibility to that level of expectation.*
>
> (Barbara, planning, 8-year organizational tenure)

> *There really is a different attitude. People are less formal. I thought people were more um . . . just more kind, more open, more relaxed, than the company I have come from, so it was a nice change. Where I was before, people were really at the arm's length kind of, the sort of snobbishness within the hierarchy. . . . When I first joined* (familyretail-addition I.S.) *it was a much flatter organization.*
>
> (Nikki, technology expert with non-managerial position, 7-year organizational tenure)

In these exemplars, both Barbara and Nikki underscore the relatively relaxed atmosphere at the company that, according to their evaluation, takes into account some of the personal preferences and needs of the organizational members. These characterizations further support the presence of the stewardship orientation in the business because of their emphasis on self-actualizing behaviors (Corbetta & Salvato, 2004). They both also refer to the strong expectations of high personal performance as a feature of business identity.

Therefore, the high accountability and results-orientation were seen as one of the defining characteristics of the business. The interviewed employees noted that the upper echelons of management within the company set high expectations for results, but also demonstrated a strong desire and determination to succeed. Even though the interviewees clearly perceived the atmosphere at the company as more friendly and laid back than at the other organizations they knew, that fact did not compromise the high expectations for each employee and the challenging nature of the work.

> *Results are the priority of the organization. . . . It's very, very requiring. Over the last 5-8 years, the requirements are more demanding of the associates here and I can say in the stores as well—they don't work 40-hr week; that's not standard anymore. People work here 12-hr days and 5-6 days a week and that's is. . . to me that's unfortunate because there is more to life than . . a job. . . . So . . . that's where it gets a little fuzzy—when you are committed to the success of your associates, that means professional success, but there is also personal success. When you drive people too hard, that takes away their personal success and level of*

> *engagement. . . . I don't know if all companies work people too hard. But I think they are headed that way. . . . If you don't meet your numbers two years in a row, as a buyer, you were most likely let go. There was very little consideration for moving you around in the company or demoting you to something. . . . You are just gone. . . . There will be examples where people have worked in the company for a very, very, very long time and there were no hesitations seemingly to let them go.*
>
> (Heather, training department, 15-year organizational tenure)

In this exemplar Heather reflects on the high results-orientation present in the business. She is of the opinion that people are forced to work too hard at the expense of their personal lives. She also wonders how this may affect their committment to the success of the organization and concludes that the employee engagement is likely to have dropped in the recent years. She hints at the tension between the espoused commitments to employees' success and the reality of forcing people to work too hard, a situation that does not allow the employees to achive success in their personal lives and also forces them to cut leisure time necessary for optimal performance on the job. In addition to that, she explains that the employees who do not meet the expectations are likely to let go, even if they worked in the business for many years. She makes that point with a sense of slight disbelief and saddness. She also explained that she has witnessed such cases first-hand as an employee working in the HR department.

The drive to be more professional than "familial" and the results-orientation was mirrored in the importance of processes and structure. Benchmarking the best practices and processes from other businesses was revealed by the interviewed employees as an important focus in the organization. At the same time, there was still a norm of approachability that, as the interviewees noted, facilitated the flow of ideas for innovation. Even though the *familyretail* structure has grown significantly in the last decades and the company was employing close to 25,000 staff, the decision-making process was expedient and efficient.

Summary of the family identity and the business identity. A few considerations related to both the family identity and the business identity of the organization emerged, which may have influenced the process of entrepreneurship in the company. In terms of the family identity, the strong determination to succeed, combined with the humility of the family members, may be important drivers of the entrepreneurial activity. The analysis of the interview data revealed that strong ambition of the family members and their drive to build a significant retail business influenced their decisions to create an ongoing innovation process, coupled with the promotion of risk-taking among the employees. By initiating these changes, they hoped to revive the organization in the face of strong competition from a host of other retailers and online stores. The norm of approachability, present within the business, facilitated the flow of ideas for innovation.

The relative humility of the family members may have influenced the lack of market aggressiveness associated with challenging the competitors directly. Throwing a gauntlet at the competitors requires a good amount of self-confidence and maybe even some arrogance. These characteristics are not the qualities of the enterprising family.

The mission of the business, defined as a dependable purveyor of clothing, grooming, and household goods, is to meet the needs of local customers. The company thus focuses on achieving that goal by constantly improving its practices. Hence, the relative absence of market proactiveness involving taking steps in anticipation of future demand and an active role in shaping customers' preferences may stem from the clarity with which the role of the business was defined. The management is proud of being servants of the customers, and they strive to continue the long company tradition in fulfilling that role. When the goal of the business and the family is to be "humble servants" delivering the customers essentials for a multitude of life's occasions, seeking entrepreneurial opportunities in the market may become a less salient goal. The business has the passion for equipping the customers with the good quality essentials; thus, all potential opportunity-seeking strategies must be fully aligned with that principle.

The family members strive to achieve the excellence of their work, which is defined more by the family managers of the business, than by the external benchmarks. In other words, the success of the business and the level of its excellence depend on the judgment of the company stakeholders. The business identity of the company defines its employees as hard-working experts that should be well-versed in the needs of the clients. The customer needs and preferences are assumed to be well understood by the organization. Consequently, entrepreneurial initiatives are focused more on collecting the ideas from the employees or "community experts" than on gathering broad-scope input from the customers. The evidence gathered as a part of this investigation revealed that the activities, such as searching, probing, and questioning—that could help "scan" the market for an opportunity and aid in being proactive in the changing retail environment—were given very little importance. Thus, with this current approach, market proactiveness as a forward-looking perspective on the market may become underdeveloped.

For any business to remain competitive in the market and relevant to its customers, the expertise of the company insiders needs constant updating. Thus, in the case of familyretail, the internal knowledge and skills may also prove inadequate, against the best wishes and the past experiences of the company experts. Moreover, with the emphasis on hard work and large workloads, the employees simply find themselves lacking time and energy for seeking new market opportunities or acting in anticipation of future demand.

Emergent finding: Community Embeddedness

One of the advantages of qualitative research is the fact that it may provide unexpected insight into processes that did not constitute the initial set of the research problems. Such was the situation in this research project. The evidence pointed to *familyretail's* long history of slow organic growth based on fulfilling the needs and using the resources present in the local community.

Closeness to the community. As large organization as *familyretail* currently is, with competitors in large cities including high-end national department stores like Macy's and Nordstrom, the company maintained a number of smaller stores that compete with local Marshalls and Kohls' in towns throughout Southeastern United States. The needs of these smaller stores are as important to the company, as the larger, higher-end stores. In the past, company growth was based on establishing partnerships with families in the community:

> *I think the company has always, from the early days forward, wanted to offer their customer value, wanted to be a solid member of the community. That's why I think the original Mr. Retailer went around and formed partnerships all over the southeast. He would take a businessman or somebody in a community that was a solid member of the community, and form a group of stores there. So, you can get embedded, you know, in- not just have a store in, but you really have embedded in the community. Like I say, you can see your partner; you'd see him in church or you'd see him at, you know, somewhere out in the city. It's uh, I think they've always wanted to be a member of the uh- felt, you know, important member of the community, and willing to give back.*
>
> (Larry, planning department, over 25 years of tenure with the company)

In this exemplar, Larry points out the close personal relationships between the company owners and their partners, who were an important component of the growth strategy for the enterprise. As Larry explains, organizational members were known members of the community, whose lives were to a large extent open to scrutiny by the community members. This transparency and constant contact with community members are likely to have created a sense of trust and connectedness, along with a conviction that the goals of the business and the community are entwined.

Community embeddedness is also expressed in one of the company's values—"Be engaged in our communities"—and is directly supported by company dedication to the community work. The available data revealed that 2.5% of company sales are dedicated to charitable work, primarily in major areas of education, and to a slightly lesser extent women's health and community building. This number was revealed by Peter, company executive with almost 30 years of organizational tenure and responsible for sales, marketing and e-commerce. Peter was insistent that 2.5% was donated based on the sales figures, not the profits, and repeated the number several times during our conversation.

This number is extraordinarily large when compared with available data on gift giving of companies in the same industry. According to the report *Giving in Numbers 2014* (Committee Encouraging Corporate Philanthropy, 2014) presenting data from world's largest companies across several industries, the median total giving in customer discretionary spending goods category was only 0.09% of sales. The purchases at a department store would fall within the discretionary spending category. The comparison between these percentages suggests that *familyretail* places very high emphasis on the charitable giving and community service.

In addition to the high company's charitable contributions, associates are also encouraged to take extra time to volunteer in their communities. As Barbara, a planner, explaned:

> *And that can especially be seen in everything we do. I mean, charity-wise. It's not just we're giving money to these places. But they're constantly encouraging us to go out into the community and to volunteer and to get involved. And that's awesome to me, to have that kind of connection to the community. And you can tell, when we go to different cities, that company has that kind of reputation, that our customer and our markets really believe that company isn't there just to screw them over. Like we're really there; we just want to be a good retailer. We want to give them good product, and we also want to help the communities we are in. So, it's nice to see that when we're out in the stores.* (Barbara)

The same sentiment was reiterated by Heather, a trainer in the HR department:

> *They want, I mean, we know that we are a southern based business, and they are going to stay very true to that, which I have the fullest respect for, um, and it just means that, they're really focusing on trying to stay true to our customer, and always bring her what she needs, what she's wanting, at the best value. Um, I think it's that focus on the customer, remaining focused on the customer, really does mean we are still trying to be that mom and pop kind of store in each of our communities, and have those relationships, and have sales associates who are genuinely friendly and helpful, and that really hearkens back to a different time in retail, it's not just about making money, it's really about a customer experience.* (Heather)

These two exemplars point to the organizational members' sense of obligation to meet an array of customers' needs, spanning from the attractive price, through the high quality, to the expert, yet caring service. Moreover, these two quotes can illustrate a sense of appreciation and respect that the organizational members have for the company leadership for applying this type of customer-focused business policy.

During the interviews, however, several employees mentioned that they saw company's emphasis on volunteering in the community as an additional obligation that took time away from their families; their attitude towards volunteering ranged between being ambivalent (they saw value of volunteering to the community) to being resentful towards the company's policy.

Emphasis on providing value for the customers. The concept of being embedded in the community included the desire to provide customers with service of high quality that took into account customers' financial considerations. Interview data analysis revealed that some of the characteristics and values of the family influenced the way business was conducted at this organization. For example, familial values of trustworthiness and being connected with the community translated into being focused on seeking value based on utility for the customers. This approach can be demonstrated in these two quotes:

> *We won't sell junk; we won't sell something overpriced. We won't sell something that we don't believe in; there's a certain quality level we won't go below. We used to do a pretty good little business, you know, the stuff you see on TV as "As Seen on TV" with us. We were selling a little bit of that, but then we got away from it. We felt like, you know, that really wasn't us. That's not really what we want the customer to think of when they think of us. We want 'em to think of solid, quality product at a good price.*
>
> (Larry, planning department, over 25 years with the company)

> *(...) our customer and our markets really believe that* familyretail *isn't there just to screw them over. Like we're really there, we just want to be a good retailer. We want to give them good product, and we also want to help the communities we are in.*
>
> (Barbara, planning, 8-year organizational tenure)

At the same time, strong profits were not the sole goal of the business. As indicated by the interviewees, compromising quality and the value for customers was not a viable option in the business economic calculation. The reputation in the community, (especially in the smaller commutities beyond large Southeastern metropolies like Atlanta or Miami) and the role of providing the community with valuable, reasonably priced goods prevented the business from selling low-quality, or low-utility items, even if they could bring high margins:

> *There's certain business we just don't go into, even though we could probably do well and make some money, because we just don't think that fits our-our atmosphere of who we are. Yeah, there- there's certain areas we won't go. . . . We just don't go down with some of the- some of the low ball stuff. We don't uh- that's just not who we are.*
>
> (Larry, planning department, over 25 years with the company)

It is important to note that in most areas *familyretail* serves communities on a budget, whose members are likely to come back to the stores if the price is right even if they had a bad experience with some of the products in the past. Thus, the focus on maintaining high quality and high value of the offerings may point out to the presence of non-economic goals present in the business that may have to do with preserving the reputation of the family, that is highly visible in the local community, especially in the Carolinas where the company is headquartered.

CHAPTER 4: DISCUSSION

While the entrepreneurial contribution of enterprising families remains largely under-researched (Cruz et al. 2006), this research addresses this gap in the management and entrepreneurship literature. The first broad research question of this study investigated how the family and non-family members influence the process of entrepreneurship in a successful transgenerational retail family business. The second broad research question focused on the influence of organizational identity on entrepreneurship and innovation in the same type of enterprise.

The results of the study indicate that the company strived to be entrepreneurial, but their efforts were inhibited by the elementary organizational pressures having to do with the lack of time and resources, as well as by some aspects of their organizational identity focused on being a community retail store. The following discussion expands on the results, as well as attempts to place them in context with the current literature on entrepreneurship in family enterprises. The last part of the discussion section aims at presenting a summary of the connections between the findings of the current case study and the extant literature on entrepreneurship in the family business, as well as develops theoretical propositions related to the questions on how and why a transgenerational family business with diminishing entrepreneurial focus may make an effort to foster entrepreneurship.

Entrepreneurial Orientation of the Business

The analysis of the innovation process revealed several important characteristics of the entrepreneurial processes at *familyretail*. These findings correspond to several recent findings on the entrepreneurship in family firms and thus have implications for the scholarship of the discipline.

Miller et al. (2011) argued that family owners and CEOs, influenced by family stakeholders in the business assume the role identity of family nurturers. They may be prone to pursue strategies of conservation, avoiding innovative, risky projects in the name of shorter-term financial security for family members. However, in the case of *familyretail* the analysis of the innovation processes strongly suggests that innovation activity has been initiated by the family members who feared that the business may be becoming obsolete in the face of rapid business environment changes and fierce competition.

The management of innovation requires deep operational knowledge that is available to both family and also to non-family employees. Both of these categories may be trusted supporters who are able to take leading roles in the identification, defense, and management of the major innovation activities of the firm (Burgelman, 1983). One of the research questions of this study was understanding the role and possible contributions of non-family employees to the entrepreneurial processes at the company. Non-family employees may be more likely than the family to have a more objective view on the company's strengths and weaknesses and thus, at least theoretically, they could be the key campaigners for business innovation. Nevertheless, in the case of this research, it was the family employees who championed the introduction of new processes, products and services at the company.

Corresponding to this result Gottschall's study (2014) found that the family employees championed a significantly greater number of the most-important innovations than non-family members. In his study, family employees originated and developed 85% of the most important innovations even though they were outnumbered by non-family employees 8.2 to 1 (Gottschall, 2014). Thus, in small family firms, non-family employees were not a significant factor on innovation.

This study supports similar conclusions. Non-family members were not the originators of entrepreneurial initiatives, even though, given the opportunity, some non-family employees joined family members in becoming champions of innovation. It is, however, necessary to mention that other employees felt overwhelmed by the scope of changes present at the company and perceived "innovation" as an additional burden placed on them by the company management. Perhaps the explanation for these findings is connected with the higher status that family members generally enjoy in the family businesses, as well as with the different informal rules of their employment. As agency theory would suggest, family members, being owners of the business may be more prone to indroduce changes and novel ideas because they are the first in line to reap the potentail benefits of innovation. At the same time, however, the possible failures of the family members have less acute consequences for their employment: Provided that the company does not go out of the market as a result of the innovation, family members are not likely to lose their jobs. Therefore, family members may have more to gain and less to lose in introducting changes in comparison with the non-family employees, whose failures may translate into a quick severance from the company.

The current research also identified innovation in the company as a highly structured process with its own delegated organizational members and resources. This may be seen as a somewhat unexpected finding. Managing family firm innovation was previously seen as a less formalized process (Moores & Mula, 2000) due to the goal congruence, possible clan-like social structures and informal communication of the family members. Also, while providing a structural support for innovation activities is important, it is highly unlikely that the innovation efforts can be successful without a change in values and norms that constitute organizational culture. This type of cultural change is likely to take a form of a more organic process.

Furthermore, there is evidence that the ideas present in a book on the innovation practices at Procter & Gamble influenced innovation at the analyzed family business. While Procter & Gamble is an important company on the US market, this finding may be perhaps aligned with the recent findings by Miller, LeBreton-Miller & Lester (2013) on the susceptibility of family firms to institutional pressures and greater willingness to adopt industry standards. This fact may be seen as a way in which family businesses strive to overcome a bias associated with a stereotypical view of family firms as "homegrown" enterprises suffering from low levels of professionalism. Therefore, a strong drive to adopt industry standards can be aimed at ameliorating these negative perceptions.

Family firms have been associated with both advantages and disadvantages in pursuing innovation (König, Kammerlander, & Enders, 2012). In correspondance with this fact, this research identified both advantages, as well as disadvantages to the entrepreneurial processes present in the discussed family business. The advantages included (1) Valuing teamwork, (2) Work content conducive to the entrepreneurial process (people felt that they worked on issues and important projects), (3) Willingness to recognize failure (not stemming from negligence) as a learning opportunity, (4) Flatter hierarchical structures that allowed ideas and solutions to be implemented rapidly without seeking consensus of multiple organizational stakeholders, (5) Encouraging employees to take risks, (6) Employees were able to express their ideas openly and honestly without the fear of reprisal; bosses were open to new initiatives coming from their collaborators, (7) Posing challenges to stimulate the search of creative solutions. Several of those advantages are also consistent with factors fostering creativity presented by Amabile (1995). These factors include organizational structures, supportive role of leaders, work content conducive to utilizing creative ideas, and autonomy that allows for the pursuit of novel solutions.

Stewardship and Long-Term Orientation

A long-term orientation is a key component of the stewardship perspective (Davis et al., 1997; Miller et al., 2008) and may explain why some family firms are more likely to invest in entrepreneurship than others (Zahra et al., 2004). The long-term orientation refers to the emphasis on patient investments with long-time horizons (e.g., Zahra et al., 2004). According to this view, family members, acting as stewards of the business, relinquish the pursuit of possible short-term gains for the long-term well-being of the firm through the costly and risky entrepreneurial activities (Eddleston et al., 2012).

Familyretail's long-term orientation can be seen as facilitating the process of change and entrepreneurship at the company. Importantly, entrepreneurship and innovation is necessary for firm continuity and is associated with long-term orientation of the business (Bhide, 2000). Consequently, long-term orientation has been deemed to have an impact on the entrepreneurial innovativeness of family firms. (Lumpkin & Brigham; 2011; Lumpkin, Brigham, & Moss; 2010).

In the analyzed business the characteristics associated with both long-term orientation and stewardship were very prominent and there is evidence that both of these features greatly influenced organizational push towards innovation. The long-term orientation has been used as a way to theoretically capture competitive performance advantages that can be enjoyed by families in business (e.g. Miller & Le-Breton Miller, 2005). Expressed in the organizational mindset of the firm and, more tangibly, through the related strategic decision-making (Lumpkin, Brigham & Moss, 2010), long-term orientation refers to the propensity of a firm to engage in long-term actions that bring potential benefits in an extended period of time (Lumpkin & Brigham, 2011). Family firms pursue conscious long-term strategies that have a direct impact on their entrepreneurial orientation, specifically on their innovativeness (Lumpkin & Brigham, 2011). New research by Diaz-Moriana et al. (2014) based on the conceptual framework of Lumpkin and Brigham (2011) found that family firms' engagement in innovation is directly related to their long-term orientation. In other words, innovative family businesses exhibited attributes associated with the long-term orientation; the findings of the current study support this pattern of linkages between the long-term orientation, stewardship and organizational innovation.

The current research found evidence of some of the aforementioned attributes. These identified attributes include investment of their own capital, longer investment horizons and a strong perseverance in reaching organizational objectives (one respondent noted that some business relationships were cultivated for decades before they brought full fruition for the organization). Transgenerational goals were expressed in general terms -"we want to be the best we can be"- rather than more specific. The long-term orientation of the business and, associated with it, strong desire to maintain the business was instrumental for implementing innovation initiatives focused on sustaining the enterprise in the increasingly competitive retail environment. Also, investment of their own capital allowed for rapidly engaging adequate funds to the benefit of change and investment initiatives.

Organizational Identity of the Business

Miller and Le Breton-Miller (2005) noted that successful family businesses tend to be "out of the mainstream" of traditional management practices in that the familial identity, as well as familial-related considerations, hold a huge sway over organizational decision-making. The firms that these researchers studied were characterized by quick decision-making practices; concern for the continuity of their mission and stewardship of the business; promoting cohesive clan cultures "shaped by authentic values, incessant indoctrination, and a deep concern for employees at all levels" (Miller & Le Breton-Miller, 2005, p. 6); and building meaningful connections with outsiders.

There are some important differences between the successful family businesses analyzed by Miller and Le Breton-Miller (2005) and the business analyzed in this study. While a number of businesses analyzed by Miller and Le Breton-Miller (2005) employed a “master-servant” arrangement for the relationship between the family and the business, the family in this study seemed to be the servant of the business (and also the customers). Thus, the business objectives were receiving priority over the potential family considerations. Nevertheless, family ideals still influenced the organization. Specifically, family values like the ethos of service, humility, unpretentiousness, and approachability influenced organizational identity, but it was the business identity that had a stronger claim on organizational identity and organizational decision-making than the identity of the family. The organization and the business seemed to have a stronger importance than the family whose role was that of “servants”, or stewards, of the business.

Also, while the organization promoted strong culture focused on customer service and involvement in communities, there was not much emphasis on clannishness or “us” relating to the family, or to the community of employees. The focus was more on the company, its current financial and organizational standing, its growth, its reputation and its future.

Nevertheless, there were also important similarities between the organization investigated in this study and the successful family businesses analyzed by Miller and Le Breton-Miller (2005). In both cases the emphasis was on the quick flow of the information, timely decision-making without negotiating with multiple organizational stakeholders (which by no means meant acting rash), concern for the continuity of mission and stewardship of the business, and reaching out to communities, both with charity work but also for advice on the business (there were innovation goals for a percentage of ideas coming from outside of the company).

The company presented in this research is likely not the only large family business surviving past the founding generation that downplays the family influence on the organization (but not necessarily the heritage, company history, etc.) and lets the business goals and business identity shape the answer to the question of who they are as an organization. The recent research of Zavattaro et al. (2014) studied organizational identities of 20 randomly selected firms from the list of America's 100 largest family firms (Pearl, 2009). These companies included both public (47%) and private organizations (53%) and represented several industries including manufacturing, retail, financial holdings, and personal care products. Zavattaro et al. (2014) found that all of these companies employed family subordination identity strategy (Micelotta & Raynard; 2011) which gives a lower profile to the familial role in the firm. Instead, the emphasis is on the company, its history, and its vision for the future.

The family subordination identity strategy is one of the three brand identity strategies classsified by Micelotta and Raynard (2011) in the time when the work on this research project was starting. These strategies can be placed on a continuum, with family preservation on one end and family subordination on the other. While family preservation strategies aim at creating an "intimate connection" (p. 202) between the family and the firm, making the two almost the same entity, the family subordination identity strategy places lower emphasis on the role of family in business, which acts as merely the guardian of the company.

Thus, the results of the current study may add yet another family business example to the collection of large family businesses where family influence is not a prominent factor influencing organizational identity. An interesting research question for future studies is whether large family organizations associate this fact with increased legitimacy, or perhaps stronger customer orientation. In addition to that, an interesting topic for the future research is also how the family subordination strategy could potentially affect stewardship attitudes, conflict management and governance in a family firm.

In addition to that, it remains open whether downplaying the family role in the business has more positive or perhaps more negative consequences for family businesses. While potential positives may include increased legitimacy and stronger governance mechanisms, there are also potential negatives. For example, Zavattaro et al. (2014) argue that family firms with family subordination brand strategy may not be fully making use of family identity that can be leveraged to improve social capital and, potentially, overall performance (Dyer, 2006). Accordingly, in the case of familyretail the family role in the business was not emphasized for many years until the family members of the current generation realized that there may be some additional "community goodwill" that can be won for the company by underscoring family history and family instrumentality in establishing, maintaining and growing the business.

Identity characteristics delineating "who we are" as a business consisting of the business-first attitude, the drive to continuously improve and to grow, avoiding being pigeonholed as old-fashioned, or being forced to change by the environment facilitated the process of organizational entrepreneurship and innovation. Even though the push toward innovation might have come as a surprise to many middle- and lower level employees who were not previously aware of the CEO's openness towards innovation, these identity characteristics facilitated a positive response from the higher-level company management.

Emergent Finding: Social Embeddedness

Social embeddedness has both to do with the story of the company's development, as well as the high level of community engagement that has been present in the business from its beginning. The company grew depending on resources of the local community, and throughout the company history until today *familyretail* business leaders feel an obligation to contribute to communities they serve.

Being engaged in the communities may be a fact that is highly advertised by business leaders in an effort to generate goodwill for company actions and offerings. However, the somewhat unexpected finding about the community engagment is that it has little, or even a negative, effect on preserving high financial performance or improving poor performance (Choi &Wang, 2009). Therefore, the fact that the company engaged in it to such a great extent may be evidence of non-economic goals present in the business focused on serving the local community. In addition to these community-centered goals, community involvement may also be associated with high socio-emotional wealth present in the business (Wiseman & Gomez-Mejia, 1998). In accordance with that fact, the presence of community involvement in the analyzed business is likely to stem from the high levels of socio-emotional wealth that the family places in the business.

Socio-emotional wealth has three components that encompass different aspects of social and emotional capital that the family members who own the business receive from maintaining it. The first component of socio-emotional wealth is family reputation. The second is family sustainability – preserving dynasty, maintaining a strong bond between the family members and keeping the business in the family. The third are family obligations which have to do with a range of tangible and intangible rewards that the family receives from the business.

Investments in positive reputational capital (Fombrun, 1996) may facilitate the attainment of economic goals for the family. For example, investments in communities allow the family and the company to build up stores of goodwill with their key stakeholders. Reserves of goodwill may act as insurance, protecting a firm's underlying relational trust and image in the marketplace, which might help sustain the company for the long-run.

Also, high socio-emotional wealth present in the business may translate into willingness to accept financial risk for the sake of preserving the sentimental value of the firm and its place in the family. Similar to long-term orientation of the business and strong desire to maintain the business, high socio-emotional wealth was probably important for innovation initiatives focused on sustaining (and not losing) the enterprise in the rapidly changing, strongly competitive retail environment.

Summary of the Possible Theoretical Implications of the Case Study

To date, no fully developed theory explains how family businesses nurture entrepreneurship (Jaskiewicz et al., 2015). Nevertheless, the research findings that have accumulated up to this point take partial steps towards theory building and point to several factors that have gained consesual support as fostering entrepreneurship in family. As a first approximation, these factors associated with entrepreneurship can be divided into family factors (e.g., family unity and family socioemotional wealth– Eddleston et al., 2012) and business factors (e.g., organizational culture – Zahra et al., 2004).

This case study contributes to the existing literature in two ways. The first contribution has to do with comparing the evidence of current case study to the evidence gathered by other family business research that investigated the topic of entrepreneurship; overall this case study offers support to the characteristics and concepts that have been associated with entrepreneurship in family businesses in previous studies.

The second contribution has to do with creating propositions based on the data analysis that attempt to go beyond what we already know about entrepreneurship in family firms. Overall, the findings of this study have implications that are most important for the future inquiry on entrepreneurship and on institutional pressures and the adoption of industry standards in family businesses.

Implications for the extant scholarship on entrepreneurship in family businesses. Previous studies have identified selected characteristics of entrepreneurship in family businesses. Current evidence suggests, that the entrepreneurial drive dissipates by the third generation (Cruz & Nordqvist, 2012; Laspita et al., 2012). The current study supports this conention by underscoring the relative lack of innovative practices, careful decision making and relative risk-avoidance that was present in the company during the leadership of the late second generation. While the third generation of family business owners introduced changes aimed at fostering innovation, these changes focused on creating a structure for organizational processes and seeked to ”import” innovative thinking originating outside of the company. Although the third generation of company business owners seeked to change organizational culture in a way that promoted more risk-taking, they failed to provide employees with adequate rewards for taking risks, or remove the possible penalties in the form of stalled careers or terminated employments. There is also evidence that the key business decisions were made primarily in the areas with strong business rationale and the company style of not dealing in anticipation of future changes on the market and not confronting the competirors directly, did not change.

Previous research has also examined the difference in influences of family members and non-family employees on entrepreneurship (Gottschall, 2014). The discussed findings suggested the primary role of family members and only supplemental role of non-family employees (Gottschall, 2014). Also, in this case the findings of this study supported previous evidence. The move towards innovation in *familyretail* was initiated by the family members. Non-family employees contributed their ideas to the innovation processes, but they were not the main champions of the innovation-focused efforts.

Existing research has also accumulated a range of factors that were deemed to foster entrepreneurship in family businesses and help to differentiate between more and less entrepreneurial family firms. These factors are presented in Table 5 along with the information on whether or not there was evidence that the concept explored in an earlier study also influenced entrepreneurship in *familyretail*. These factors are discussed in more detail futher on.

Table 5: Factors facilitating entrepreneurship in family businesses

Concept or descriptive factor	Extant research	Evidence of significance in *familyretail*
Long-term orientation	Ogbonna and Harris, 2001	Yes
Family financial capital	Aldrich et al., 1998	Yes
Family social capital	Sorensen, 2007	Yes
Aspects of stewardship and socioemotional wealth	Eddleston et al., 2012	Yes

The findings of this research suggest that stewardship attitudes towards the business along with a long-term orientation focused on company survival and growth prompted the leaders of *familyretail* to embark on an initiative supporting innovative projects and more risk-taking within the business.

With regard to other factors facilitating entrepreneurship, it may also be notable that *familyretail* family members possessed adequate financial resources, mainly in the form of cash, that aided the discussed organizational change. Also in this case, current research accumulated evidence that the financial resources of the family provided for more speedy implementation of innovatively focused organizational changes.

Moreover, family social capital may also be seen an important correlate and possibly a driver of entrepreneurship because business preservation and renewal is often an important factor in preserving high social status of the family. The business family of this study was one of the most prominent families in the region, possessing a significant amount of social capital, which was associated to a great extent with being the owners of a large, well-known business in the region. Therefore, maintaining the social capital of the family was dependent on the survival and prosperity of the business. High social capital of *familyretail* family, as well as the motivation to preserve that familial asset, may be seen some of the drivers for increased entrepreneurship in the company.

All together, I propose that the factors presented in Table 5 are important because they help explain key characteristics that make some family firms more entrepreneurial than others. However, they do not explain why a transgenerational family business with diminishing entrepreneurial focus might make an effort to foster entrepreneurship for the sake of maintaning competitiveness. Futhermore, these factors do not explain how a family business may choose to implement this change. I believe that the evidence of this case study may allow creating propositions on how these processes may transpire. These propositions are discussed in the following section.

Theoretical propositions. The findings of this study may allow one to create propositions on how a transgenerational family business may adopt practices consistent with a more entrepreneurial business orientation. The first hypothesized process is outlined below in Figure 1. The proposed process relates to a transgenerational family business with long tenure on the market, exactly the situation of the business studied in this research. Long company tenure is associated with an increase of environmental pressures that may threaten the survival of the enterprise. Third generation of *familyretail* business owners faced challenges associated with rapidly evolving industry. At the same time, the business did not possess internal mechanisms that would help it adapt to these new circumstances. Organizational culture, as known by the majority of employees who did not constitute the nearest circles of the enterprising family, did not recognize change, adaptation, innovation, or risk-taking as important organizational values; *familyretail* business owners were risk conscious with the propensity to make well-conceived business decisions.

The push and pull theory of motivation for entrepreneurship suggest that there are different factors that motivate people to pursue entrepreneurial activities (Bird, 1989). *Pull* factors are construed as the positive forces; they include a passion for creativity, a desire to make own mark in a family enterprise, or an organizational culture for innovation and creativity (Hoy & Sharma, 2010; Shapiro, 1975). The *push* factors, on the other hand, have to do with a necessity to introduce changes due to changes in the competitive landscape leading to a need to redefine the business if it is to survive (Hoy & Sharma, 2010; Shapiro, 1975). The evidence of this case study may suggest that the importance of pull factors wanes as family enterprises age and the organizational culture for innovation and entrepreneurship decreases; on the other hand, the significance of push factors waxes as the competitive environment changes with time. In this case study it was the push factors that prompted the third generation of the family members currently at the helm of the business to make a broad effort to introduce more innovation to the company.

The evidence of this study may also support that the stewardship attitudes and socioemotional wealth that the family had invested in the business may have facilitated the process of adopting entrepreneurially-minded practices. It is generally assumed in the literature on family business that protecting socioemotional wealth encourages risk-averse decisions (Chrisman et al., 2012; Gómez-Mejía et al., 2007). Socioemotional wealth is the sum of all affective benefits that a family derives from their control of the enterprise. It includes preserving dynastic family control (Gómez-Mejía et al., 2007), offering employment and other resources for family members (Schulze et al., 2003), building the family's reputation in the community (Deephouse & Jaskiewicz, 2013), as well as investing in community-focused activities (Berrone et al., 2010). However, it may be argued that in the case of this study, protecting socioemotional wealth encouraged family members to introduce more innovation and increase the overall entrepreneurial orientation of the business in the face of an acute threat to the company survival.

The findings of this study may also cast light on the mode in which family businesses may attempt to instill a more entrepreneurial focus into aging transgenerational companies where an entrepreneurial approach has not been cultivated since the early stages of its existance. The evidence of this study suggests that the way of introducing innovative thinking into the business was focused largely on best practices developed in the corporate setting, which may indicate a strong influence of institutionalized structures and norms present in the market environment. It is important to note that in this case study the family business did not focus primarily on making decisive changes to the organizational culture, or equipping employees with more discretion for introducing innovative solutions, focused instead on creating structural support for innovation and codifying the rules for entrepreneurial practices. Provided that there is evidence that family businesses may be more prone than other businesses to adopt institutionalized industry standards (Miller, LeBreton-Miller & Lester, 2013), this study may provide evidence that the institutionalized pressures may also play a role in the way family businesses endeavor to be more entrepreneurial.

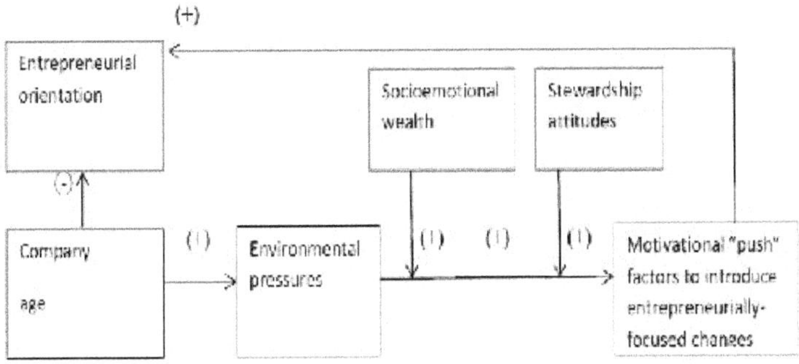

Figure 1: Model of the process of how a transgenerational family business may adopt practices consistent with a more entrepreneurial orientation

The second hypothesized process is outlined below in Figure 2. The lack of strong competitors and high demand for essential goods in a relatively underserved area of rural North Carolina created a unique business oportunity for the first generation of *familyretail* business owners. The first generation adjusted their business strategy to the characteristics of the local market. The owners focused on keeping the prices low, and made sure that the products met the quality requirements of local farmers. Their efforts led to early success and growth of the business.

During the time of first and second generations, business conditions did not change significantly with regard to the characteristics of market demand and the number of competitors. According to Porter (1990), business rivalry and the nature of customer demand represent the essential pressures that force companies to be innovative. In the case of *familyretail*, neither customers expectations, nor tastes, changed significantly in the geographic area where the business was growing; customers' needs remained focused on mid-range quality essentails. Importantly, with regard to the competitive landscape, department stores experienced significant consolidation, that accelerated after II World War (Hix, 2014), which weakened the competitive pressures present in the industry. With the consolidation of the department stores, the companies started carrying similar product offerings and the department stores also started looking more and more similar to each other (Hix, 2014). This created an environment in which change happened slowly and innovation was not essentail for the survival of the enterprise. The company chose their market strategy to be based on replicating the successful business model. There was little need of changing that model in a significant way.

During the leadership of the second generation there were only two major changes in campany operations. Those changes were relatively minor from the perspective of company strategy, and they nature can underscore, how little had been changing in the competitive landscape of the department store business. The first change came in the 60's when *familyretail* decided to move its flagship downtown location to a mall in the growing city suburbs. This move was, however, consistent with the decisions made by department stores across the country, as the social unrest of the Civil Rights Movement deterred women from visiting downtown shopping centres (Whitaker, 2011). The second change came when *familyretail* consolidated its ownership as the old ownership structure become increasingly untenable; in 1998, the company formed a new legal entity that merged over a hundred *familyretail* companies, swapping the existing partners' local interests for shares in the combined entity.

The first important changes in the competitive environment came in the first decade of XXI century when the competitive pressures from other (especially online) retailers became much stronger and the demand for higher-end products increased in *familyretail's* headquarters location. These changes increased the competitive pressures on the business, as well as impacted the expectatations of local customers with regard to the products, as well as the services. Until those changes, the company did not face a strong need to change, adopt and innovate.

During the time of the first two generations of company leadership the growth strategy was focused on replicating the successful strategy of gaining the market share by opening additional stores that had very similar product offerings and catered to the same category of the core middle-class clientele. Importantly, the growth was not being achieved by adjusting the services to changing customer needs, or the pressure from other retailers in the same segment of the market; neither was the effort placed in gaining a clearer or earlier picture on changing buyer trends. While the market rivalry and demand conditions remained relatively constant, the company pursued growth using a risk-averse strategy: Achieving greater market share by opening more stores in the same or similar geographic area made it easier for the family business to survive in times of market downturns, and, importantly, allowed the family members to protect the illiquid equity in the business. Replicating the established business model, weak market competition and unchanging demand conditions with the emphasis on essentials, influenced the organizational culture present in the company in a way that limited the emphasis on innovation and risk-taking. The potentail rewards of entrepreneurial orientation, like innovating with services and products, screening the market for clues about changing buyer's needs, or challenging the competitors directly, were too small to be taken into account when making business decisions.

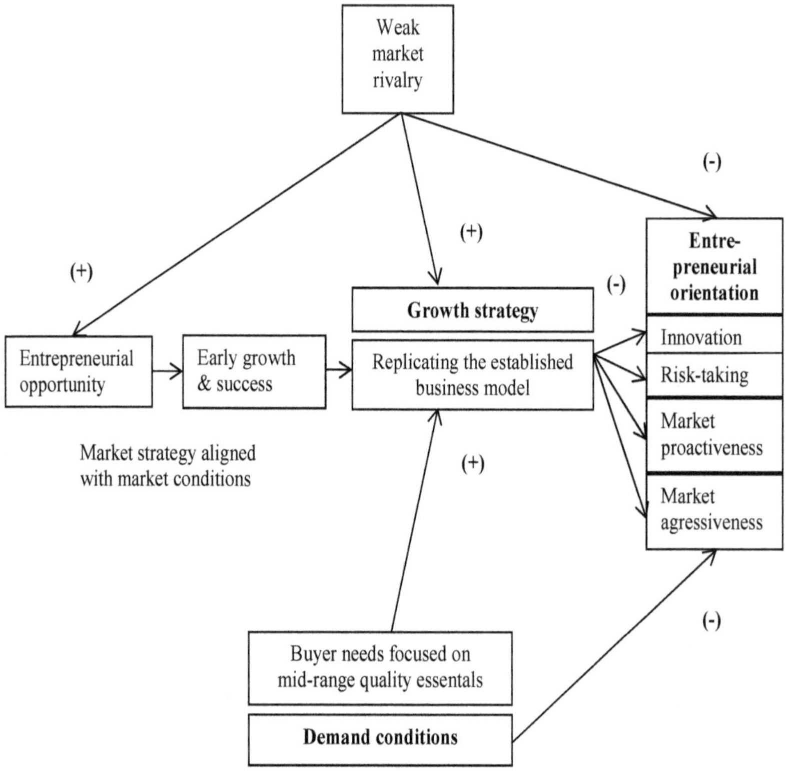

Figure 2: Model of factors that impacted the implementation of a risk-avoidant growth strategy and contributed to the low entrepreneurial orientation present in *familyretail.*

Implications for Practice

This study corroborates the body of research on family businesses that has concluded that these entities are a unique organizational form because of the family's presence. The results of this study emphasize that the meaning and the value that the family places on the business are important factors in family firm decision-making. At the same time this study also illustrates how innovation practices from non-family organizations may be implemented and utilized in the context of family businesses.

The company that was the subject of this study excelled at creating structures for the innovation process, but failed, however, to provide workers with adequate time, human resources and, partially incentives for introducing novel business solutions. Therefore, the content of this study may provide the family business owners and family business practitioners a lens through which they can gain understanding of employees' frustrations and dilemmas engendered by these circumstances. Family business owners and family business consultants need to pay special attention to the need of assuring adequate time and human resources , so that the innovative processes can be fully effective. This recommendation is relevant to all businesses, but it may be of special importance to family businesses, which, due to their careful financial management and unwillingness to use debt financing, may struggle with limited resources.

Specifically, *familyretail* created a website where employees left hundreds of novel ideas for company improvement. Even though many employees felt their ideas did not receive enough attention due to limited resources, the website as platform for gathering employee feedback was a major success. In a sense, the communication bottleneck effect was caused by the huge popularity of the website that became the victim of its own success. Thus, creating engaging forms of connection that facilitate communication and the flow of ideas is an important factor for family business entrepreneurship. Similar to the company analyzed in this study, family businesses can create their own websites and social media structures connecting family members as well as the employees. The benefit of these forms is staying connected and current with each other. However, it is also important to allocate appropriate resources to monitor and provide feedback to the authors of the posts; all projects developed on these platforms need to have their assigned champions so that all parties can clearly see the impact of their efforts.

Moreover, business owners have to be very cognizant of the messages sent to the employees with regard to the possibly negative outcomes of the risk-taking: Employees need to be assured that risks that prove unsuccessful will not cause a termination of their employment. Inspiring risk-taking is an important force for entrepreneurship that can be utilized in the family business context. It is important, however, not only to ameliorate the negative perceptions of failure, but also to address the vital concerns of the employees: To assure them that business choices that do not "work" will not be the cause for stalled or broken careers.

The findings of this study also underscore that family businesses are capable of developing risk-taking practices that allow enterprises to take "baby steps" and reduce negative consequences of financial costs associated with ventures that do not work. This approach of using limited financial resources for novel projects may be particularly appealing to family business owners, many of whom try to limit their financial exposure to risks.

Moreover, having all the advantages for the innovation process in mind, the company could also do more to help people devote sufficient time to the pursuit of new opportunities; several respondents in buying and planning offices mentioned workload levels that did not allow them to devote time to innovation activities. It is important that the process of reviewing employee's novel ideas and giving feedback is reorganized so that workers can receive more feedback on their efforts and see more ideas implemented. A fully-fledged innovation strategy focused on addressing the issues concerning inadequate resources for innovation could go a long way in improving employees' "buy-in" and increasing the productivity of all of the innovation structures already in place in the company.

Familyretial is a business highly involved in the local community and the current generation of family members at the helm of the company has started exploiting its history and the close connection with the local region in advertising. While this strategy presents and important opportunity for *familyretail's* marketing efforts, it may also come at a cost of losing authenticity in the eyes of the customers. This is so because the customers may reason that the charitable work that has been done for years without being known to the public, and thus, without an expectation of rewards, is now being done, at least in part, with the hope of improving the bottom line. It is, thus, important how the company addresses this possible issue in communication with the clients. Therefore, when publicizing the fact of being a family company with important ties to the region, it would be advisable to explain to the customers why this fact matters for their experience at stores, and how it affects company mission and values. *Familyretial* leaders care about the local community not just through the charitable work, but their community-centered intentions are also reflected in their approach to providing high-level customer service and quality goods for customers with limited budget. Providing this context may go a long way in generating goodwill for the company.

Limitations

Every study has limitations that can potentially render the results less reliable and thus decrease their usefulness for theory building and applications in practice. In this study I tried to distinguish factors stemming from the interaction between the family and non-family organizational members that allowed the business to survive and grow in spite of a difficult market environment in retail industry. One of the limitations of this study is the fact that I did not interview the two family members currently managing the company. I did, however, interview one family member who used to work in the business for a period of roughly 10 years and is currently managing *familyretail* charitable foundation. I have also interviewed people close to the family, all of whom remained in constant contact with the family members for at least 15 years.

The analyzed business has also a number of idiosyncratic characteristics that may prevent the results of the study to be applied for understanding of other family businesses. *Familyretail* is a department store, a business in the retail industry that is currently under strong competitive pressures, and that has also been weakened by the downturn in the economy following the events of the 2008 failure in the US banking system. As Eisenhardt (1989) points out, there is a danger of idiosyncratic cases preventing the analyst from raising the level of generality of the theory. It is possible that, that idiosyncrasies of a particular case may become over-interpreted and acquire too much of a central focus in the theory-building (Eco, 1992; Eisenhardt, 1989, p. 547).

CHAPTER 5: CONCLUSIONS

There are several conclusions of this study. The first conclusion to note is the fact that this research provided evidence of a family business being able to launch a program focused on increasing innovation and risk-taking and achieve meaningful results. The analyzed business devoted great resources to create a program focused on increasing the innovation and risk-taking. This approach was undertaken with an aim to revitalize the business and the attempt was influenced by the feelings of stewardship over the deteriorating company. The leaders of the company were able to create a range of structural mechanisms supporting innovation, accumulate great number of improvement ideas from the employees, as well as launch several projects based on the feedback to innovation challenges and ideas received from the workers. Even though the innovation efforts were inhibited by the lack of resources and the strong organizational identity centered on being a retail community store that limited the range of possible new ventures, the company was able to make some advances with new products and processes, as well as start the conversation with the employees on the importance and the meaning of innovation and risk-taking.

The second important conclusion of this research study is the fact that the family members may be more active in innovation efforts than non-family members. In the analyzed business family members were the originators of the entrepreneurially-focused initiatives. As one of the hypotheses of this research I theorized that the non-family members may view the business through a more objective lens than the family, and thus the non-family employees may be more inclined to propose changes to company assortment and operations. This supposition was not supported by the evidence. While some non-family employees were very active supporters (even self-described "fans") of the innovation efforts, the family members were the initiators and ultimate champions of innovation in the company.

The third conclusion of this research project is the fact that programs focused on increasing innovation and risk-taking require human resources and constant management in order to succeed. In other words, programs focused on increasing innovation and risk-taking require champions: Groups of people who evaluate ideas and provide feedback to the idea originators. A novel idea without follow-up may not only be a missed business opportunity, but may also equal a disgruntled employee. Even though the company has a team devoted to innovation, this team consists of only three full-time employees; for the other employees, innovation-related responsibilities create an added workload that is separate from their main responsibilities. Human time and effort in the form of oversight and maintenance of communication lines between different organizational members constitute important resources needed for innovation.

The fourth conclusion of this research project is the fact that the non-family employees working in family businesses may not be aware of some of the values and attitudes of the family members at the helm of the company. At the same time, the family members at the higher echelons of the organization may not be fully cognizant of the organizational culture that is present in the business. In the case of the analyzed business, family members, as well as people close to the family circle, reported that the previous company CEO placed a high value on change, experimentation and constant adjustment to customer preferences. The rest of the company employees, however, including those with a long organizational tenure, were unaware of such attitudes. Innovation seemed for them to be an imported concept. They also lacked defined notions of the meaning of the innovation. This fact may suggest that there may be a significant disconnect between what the family members imagine organizational culture to be and what information is available to the employees.

Another important conclusion of this research project is the fact that family businesses may suffer from "inferiority complexes" dictating that the best practices reside within large corporations. Several respondents in this study estimated that the company management may have felt that their company was not as established as the competitors' companies. In addition to that, during the time when innovation activities were implemented, the management was also focused on recruiting talent from large, publicly traded department stores. These types of attitudes may significantly affect the company. The lack of self-assurance may negatively influence all aspects of entrepreneurial orientation from the level of innovation, through the risk-taking and the forward-looking perspective on the market, to the aggressiveness towards the competitors. The propensity to "borrow" knowledge and best practices from larger companies may curb self-reflection on the best approaches and the steady self-improvement of business practices. In addition to that, the possible "inferiority complexes" of family businesses may particularly negatively influence non-family employees, especially those with long organizational tenures. While the family members enjoy a relatively high status in their businesses, non-family employees who have spent a long time with the company may be seen as potentially less qualified than people working outside of the family business. Thus, the talents and contributions of non-family members, especially those who worked in family businesses for a long time, may become undervalued.

The final conclusion of this study is that family businesses may be deeply embedded in their communities and may be more prone to include community-centered considerations in their decision-making. This research found a special, long-term relationship between the family business described in this study and its community. The business grew based on community networks. The community service and charitable contributions were important values for the enterprising family, the fact that has been publicized only under current leadership of the company. Also, the community involvement and charitable work allowed the business to build a significant amount of goodwill. An interesting research question for future studies would be how the community embeddeddness impacted different facets of organizational decision-making.

The conclusions of this study may provide evidence that qualitative research in family businesses can be an effective tool for gaining insight into the organizational processes at play in this type of enterprises. It is the richness, the complexity and the depth of the qualitative data that with, proper aggregation and successive testing, can make the theories stronger and more relevant.

www.ingramcontent.com/pod-product-compliance
Lightning Source LLC
Chambersburg PA
CBHW071352230926
51846CB00002B/521

* 9 7 8 4 6 1 6 9 3 6 7 9 3 *